French Grammar
For Beginners

The most complete textbook and
workbook for French Learners
By Frederic Bibard

Table of Contents

A FOREWORD

French is the second most widely taught foreign language in the world. Weirdly, however, and despite the staggering amount of material available on the topic, there is a distinct lack of resources that approach the subject in a fun and lively manner.

This is the glaring omission I attempt to cover in my website, the subsequent emails, news-letters, and of course, this book. Since the conception of my website www.talkinfrench.com, my team and I have endeavoured to approach learning French in an unconventional way by making it engaging, friendly, and injected with a little bit of humour here and there.

What others call 'tried-and-tested', I call 'old and boring', and I am trying my best to do away with it even if it kills me (figuratively speaking, of course).

Let's face it, learning a new language is hard. I'm not going to sugarcoat my words and say that you'll breeze through it all like the genius that you are. Well, I could be wrong and you could be a genuine linguistic genius of some sort. But definitely, not everyone is.

To achieve a certain level of fluency in a language, the average person has to study it for at least 800 hours. This length of time can seem unbearable to a lot of people and the tendency to quit when the going gets tough and boring is high. To prevent this, I want you to build a habit for learning French. Together, we can work hand in hand to achieve this. Moreover, once you have created the learning habit, I assure you, it only gets easier.

This book is structured in such a way that habit-creation and fun are carefully combined and lovingly married together to create a gorgeous offspring known as language learning. (Are you excited yet? I sure am.)

I hope you'll join us for this one heck of a ride. So come on, get on board with me for thirty days and let's make learning French a habit.

à bientôt!

Frederic, Founder of Talkinfrench.com

Important note: If you want the audio, go to page 174.

Day 1: Les Salutations. Greetings.

LESSON 1: French Greetings

...or how a quick smile is never enough.

Greetings are amongst one of the very first things you should consider when learning a new language. Whether a trip to a French-speaking destination is on the horizon for you or not, you should always be armed and ready with these indispensable words.

In some countries, smiling or nodding your head in acknowledgment can already be considered a form of greeting. This is not the case in French. The polite way to go about your day is to utter a quick hello to everyone you come across, including everyone within earshot in public places. Each conversation is also expected to begin with a proper greeting.

Ready yet? Here are the greetings that, like the native French, should be second nature to you too.

Track 1 (you can download the audio page 185

Bonjour!	[bohn-zoor]	Hello!
		Good morning! Good day!
Bonsoir!	[bohn-swar]	Good Evening!
Salut!	[sa-lew]	Hello/Hi! (informal)

Aside from the usual 'hellos', it is also quite common to ask 'how's it going' or 'how are you'.

Comment ça va?	[koh-mmahn-sah-vah]	How are things? How's it going?
Comment vas tu?	[koh-mmahn-vah-too]	How are you? (informal)
Comment allez-vous?	[kohn-mmahn-t-ahlaayvoo]	How are you? (formal)
Ça va?	[sah-vah]	How's it going? (informal)

And this is how you reply.

Bien, merci.	[bee-anh mair-see]	Well, thank you.
Très bien.	[tray bee-anh]	Very well.
Tout va bien.	[too vah bee-anh]	Everything is going well.
Pas très bien.	[pah tray bee-anh]	Not very well.
Pas trop mal.	[pah trow mahl]	Not too bad.

After replying, you should also ask how the other person is doing. You can do this by simply saying:

| Et toi? | [eh toa] | And you? (informal) |
| Et vous? | [eh voo] | And you? (formal) |

When you've exhausted all the 'hi's' and 'hello's' and it's time to move on, here's what you can say.

Au revoir!	[oh ruh-vwar]	Goodbye!
Salut!	[sah-loo]	Bye! (informal)
À bientôt!	[ah bianh-toh]	See you soon!
Bonne journée!	[bonn zhoor-nayh]	Good day! Have a nice day!
Bonne nuit!	[bohn-nwee]	Good night! (used only when you're about to go to sleep)

And finally,

Kissing the cheeks is also expected, but only if you are already familiar with the person. If you're meeting him or her for the very first time, you're better off simply shaking hands. Now, the number of kisses can be quite confusing. In Paris, it's generally four, but in the rest of France, it's two. In other French-speaking countries, it also varies. The best thing to do is just observe before you dive ahead.

LET'S PRACTICE!

Exercise 1.1 - Fill in the blanks in this dialogue:

Formal discussion (your boss):

Vous (you): ...*Bonjour*... Monsieur!

Votre chef (your boss): Bonjour, *Comment allez*? *vous*

Vous (you): ...*Bien*..., et vous?

Votre Chef (your boss): *Bien*..., merci.

Informal discussion (friends):
Vous (you): *Salut*!

Votre ami (your friend): Salut XXX, ...*Ça va*...?

Vous (you): Oui ca va, ...*Merci*...?

Votre ami (your friend): *Salut*..., bonne journée.

Fun fact: *French is the second most widely taught foreign language in the world after English.*

Exercise 1.2 - Choose the correct answer:

1- Rachel is a friend of Marie. She would tell her:
   a. Comment vas-tu?   b. Comment allez-vous?

2- It's morning. Paul wants to say good morning to Mark. He would say:
   a. Bonsoir!   b. Bonne journée.   c. Bonjour!

3- To wish someone good night, you would say:
   a. Bonsoir!   b. Bonne nuit.   c. Bonne journée!

4- To say goodbye, you should say:
   a. Salut!   b. Ça va?   c. Au revoir.

5- You want to ask your boss how he is, you say:
   a. Comment vas-tu?   b. Comment allez-vous?

Exercise 1.3 - Translate from French to English and vice versa:

French	English
1- Bonjour!	*Good Morning*
2- ...... *Comment Ca va*	How are things?
3- ...... *Bien Merci*	Well, Thank you.
4- Pas très bien.	*not very well*
5- ...... *Et tu*	And you? (informal)
6- Au revoir.	*Good bye*

Exercise 1.4 - This is a conversation between you and a friend (informal). Make the necessary changes so that it becomes a conversation between you and your boss (formal):

Vous (you): Salut! Comment ~~vas-tu?~~ *allez vous*

Votre ami (your friend): Bien. Et ~~toi?~~ *vous*

Vous (you): Pas mal. À bientôt! *au revoir*

Votre ami (your friend): Salut!

Exercise 1.5 - Translate from French to English and vice versa:

French	English
1- ...... *Bon nuit*	Good evening.
2- ...... *Ça va*	How are you? (informal)
3- Très bien.	...... *very well*
4- ...... *Pas trop mal*	Not too bad.
5- .... *Et vous*	And you? (formal)
6- À bientôt!	...... *See you later*

Exercise 1.6 - Translate this conversation from English to French:

You: Good morning. How's it going? *Bonjour Comment ça*

Your friend: Not too bad. And you? *Pas trop mal Et toi? va*

You: Everything is going well. See you soon! *Tout va bien à bientôt*

Your friend: Bye! *Salut*

Exercise 1.7 - Choose the correct answer.

1- Your friend asked you "Ça va?". You're not feeling very well, you would say:

    a. Très bien.   b. Pas trop mal.   c. Pas très bien.

2- To wish someone a good day, you would say:

    a. Bonne journée!   b. Bonne nuit!   c. Bonjour!

3- You've been talking to a friend and you want to say "see you soon" before going your separate ways, you would say:

    a. Au revoir!   b. À bientôt!   c. Salut!

4- You're talking to your boss. You would say:

    a. Je vais bien, merci. Et toi?   b. Je vais bien, merci. Et vous?

5- How would you answer if somebody asked you "Comment ça va?":

    a. Très bien, merci.   b. Salut!   c. Au revoir.

Exercise 1.8 - Translate from French to English and vice versa:

French	English
1- ……. *Salut*	Hello/Hi! (informal)
2- …… *Comment allez-vous*	How are you? (formal)
3- Tout va bien.	…… *Everything is well*
4- …… *Salut*	Bye! (informal)
5- Bonne nuit.	…… *Good night*
6- Bonne journée.	*Have a nice day*

Exercise 1.9 - Translate this conversation from French to English:

Vous: Bonjour Monsieur. Comment allez-vous? *Hello sir. How are you*

Votre patron: Bien, merci. Et vous? *Good thank you. And you*

Vous: Tout va bien, merci. Au revoir. *Everything is going well. Thank you*

Votre patron: Bonne journée. *Have a nice day* *good day*

ANSWERS:

Exercise 1.1 - Track 2

Formal discussion (your boss):

Vous (you): Bonjour Monsieur!

Votre chef (your boss): Bonjour, comment allez-vous?

Vous (you): Très bien merci, et vous?

Votre Chef (your boss): Très bien, merci.

Informal discussion (friends):

Vous (you): Salut!

Votre ami (your friend): Salut XXX, ça va?

Vous (you): Oui ca va, et toi?

Votre ami (your friend): Pas mal, bonne journée.

Exercise 1.2

1/ Comment vas-tu? 2/ Bonjour! 3/ Bonne nuit! 4/Au revoir. 5/Comment allez-vous?

Exercise 1.3

1/ Good morning! or Hello! 2/Comment ça va? 3/Bien, merci. 4/Not very well. 5/Et toi? 6/ Goodbye.

Exercise 1.4 (Possible Answer)

1/ Bonjour. Comment allez-vous? 2/ Bien, merci. Et vous ? 3/ Bien. Bonne journée. 4/ Au revoir.

Exercise 1.5

1/ Bonsoir. 2/Comment vas-tu? 3/Very well. 4/ Pas trop mal. 5/Et vous? 6/See you soon!

Exercise 1.6

1/ **Vous:** Bonjour. Ça va? 2/ **Votre ami:** Pas trop mal. Et toi? 3/ **Vous:** Tout va bien. A bientôt! 4/**Votre ami:** Salut!

Exercise 1.7

1/ Pas très bien. 2/ Bonne journée! 3/ À bientôt! 4/ Je vais bien, merci. Et vous? 5/ Très bien, merci.

Exercise 1.8

1/ Salut! 2/ Comment allez-vous? 3/ Everything is going well. 4/ Salut! 5/ Good night. 6/ Have a nice day.

Exercise 1.9

You: Good morning Sir. How are you? / **Your boss:** Well, thank you. And you? / **You:** Everything is going well, thank you. Goodbye. / **Your boss:** Have a nice day.

Day 2: Les Articles. The Articles.

LESSON 2: Articles

....or how it all begins.

You are already familiar with articles in sentence structures. These are the little words that appear before a noun, announcing their presence, and letting you know beforehand how many there are, and what the gender of the noun is. In English, we don't need to bother with the gender, but that's where it gets interesting in French.

> As a tip, I suggest that when you start listing nouns for your French vocabulary, you should include the articles on your list. This would make memorizing the gender of the nouns a lot easier.

There are three kinds of articles in French: definite, indefinite, and partitive.

Here's how they differ.

Definite articles are specific. **Indefinite articles** are not.

Partitive articles are used for unknown quantities or uncountable things.

In English, the definite article is 'the'. Indefinite articles are 'a' and 'an' or 'some' for the plural. Partitive articles don't exist in English, but the closest translation would be 'some' or 'any'.

French articles are more widely used than their English peers.

- **Le, la, les (articles définis)**

Remember: **Le** is for masculine singular nouns. **La** is for feminine singular nouns. **Les** is for plural nouns, regardless of whether they are male or female.

If the noun being presented starts with a vowel or a mute **h**, **le** or **la** is shortened into **l'**.

Some examples:

Track 3

le chien	(the dog)	les chiens (the dogs)
la reine	(the queen)	les reines (the queens)
l'ami	(the friend)	les amis (the friends)
l'homme	(the man)	les hommes (the men
le hamster*	(the hamster)	les hamsters (the hamsters)

Exercise 2.1 - Fill in the blanks with [le], [la], [les] or [l']:

1- _Le_ chien de mon voisin est mignon. (my neighbour's dog is cute.)

2- _L'_ ami de mon frère est aussi mon ami. (My brother's friend is also my friend.)

3- Passe-moi _l'_eau s'il te plait. (Pass me the water please.)

4- _Les_ enfants jouent dehors. (The children are playing outside.)

5- _La_ maman de mon ami est gentille. (My friend's mom is nice.)

- **Un, une, des (articles indéfinis)**

Remember: **un** is for masculine singular nouns. **une** is for feminine singular nouns. **des** is for plural nouns, whether male or female.

Some examples:

Track 4

un chien	(a dog)	des chiens (some/any dogs)
une reine	(a queen)	des reines (some/any queens)
un ami	(a friend)	des amis (some/any friends)

When an indefinite article is used in a negative sentence (ne... pas), **un, une,** and **des** are replaced with **de**. *De* changes to **d'** when used with nouns that begin with a vowel or the mute **h**.

- **Du, de la, des (articles partitifs)**

Remember: **du** is for masculine singular nouns. **de la** is for feminine singular nouns. **des** is for plural and doesn't matter if the nouns are male or female or what letter they begin with.

If the noun being presented starts with a vowel or a mute **h, du** or **de la** becomes **de l'** regardless of the gender.

Some examples:

Track 5

du gâteau	(some/any cake)	des gâteaux (some/any cakes)
de la viande	(some/any meat)	des viandes (some/any meats)
de l'argent (masculine)	(some/any money)	/
de l'herbe (feminine)	(some/any grass)	des herbes (some/any grasses)

Exercise 2.2 - Fill in the blanks with [un] or [une], [des] or [de]:

1- Je veux adopter ____ chien. (I want to adopt a dog.)

2- J'ai acheté ____ nouvelle maison. (I bought a new house.)

3- Il a acheté ____nouvelles chaussures. (He bought new shoes.)

4- Elle mange ____ pommes. (She's eating apples.)

5- J'ai trouvé ____ chat dans la rue. (I found a cat in the street.)

LET'S PRACTICE SOME MORE!

Exercise 2.3 - Put the right article in the following exercices:

1- C'est ____ chien. (It is a dog.)

2- C'est ____ fille. (It is a girl.)

3- Ce sont ____ livres. (Those are books.)

4- C'est ____ maison de Sophie. (This is the house of Sophie.)

5- C'est ____ livre de Jean. (It is the book of Jean.)

6- Ce sont ____ chocolats de Patrick. (Those are the chocolates of Patrick.)

Fun fact: *The Eiffel Tower is repainted every 7 years.*

Exercise 2.4 - Fill the blanks with the correct definite or indefinite article "le/la/l'" or "un/une"

1- Le Japon, c'est __ pays où ils ont fait tous leurs vies. (Japan is the country where they made all their lives.)

2- Est-ce qu'il y a __ poste dans ce village? (Is there a post office in this village?)

3- À droite, c›est __ chambre des parents. À gauche, …. salon. En face, …. chambre des enfants. Il y a __ salle de bains au premier étage. (On the right is the parents' room. On the left, the living room. Opposite, the children's room. There is the bathroom on the first floor.)

4- Tu connais __ mère de Pierre? (Do you know Pierre's mother?)

5- J'habite dans __ rue de l'Amour. (I live in the rue de l'Amour.)

6- J'ai stationné __ voiture à la gare. (I parked the car at the station.)

7- Voici la clef qui permet d'ouvrir __ chambre. C'est …. numéro 47. (This is the key that opens the room. It's number 47.)

8- Nous habitons sur __ place centrale du village. (We live in the central square of the village.)

9- J'aime beaucoup __ soleil, __ mer et __ sable. (I love the sun, the sea and the sand.)

10- Arles, c'est __ ville très sympathique. (Arles is a very nice city.)

Exercise 2.5 - Put the right articles in the following sentences:

1- C'est __ livre. (It's a book.)

2- C'est __ chocolat. (It's chocolate.)

3- C'est __ fille. (It's a girl.)

4- Ce sont __ biscuits. (Those are biscuits.)

5- Ce sont __ biscuits de Marie. (Those are Marie's biscuits.)

Exercise 2.6 - Put these articles in the right column : le, un, des, les, une, de la, la, des, du:

Articles définis	Articles indéfinis	Articles partitifs

Exercise 2.7 - Put the right articles in the following sentences :

1- Paris est __ capitale de La France. (Paris is the capital of France.)

2- Jean est __ bon garçon. (Jean is a good boy.)

3- Je bois __ jus d'orange. (I drink orange juice.)

4- J'achète __ cadeaux pour ma famille. (I buy gifts for my family.)

5- Caroline aime __ animaux. (Caroline likes animals.)

Exercise 2.8 - Tick the right answer:

1- Il mange __ poire. (He eats a pear.)

   a. une   b. un   c. la

2- Il prépare __ gateau. (He's making a cake.)

   a. le   b. un   c. du

3- J'ai regardé __ film au cinéma. (I watched a movie at the cinema.)

   a. une   b. des   c. un

4- __ enfants de ma soeur sont gentils. (My sister's children are nice.)

   a. des   b. de la   c. les

5- J'ai offert __ fleurs à ma maman. (I offered flowers to my mom.)

   a. les   b. des   c. une

Exercise 2.9 - Put the right articles in the following sentences :

1- Elle boit __ lait. (She's drinking milk.)

2- Frank est __ meilleur ami de François. (Frank is François's best friend.)

3- "__ reine des neiges" est un bon film. ("Frozen" (the snow queen) is a good movie.)

4- Il m'a prêté __ argent. (He lent me money.)

5- J'ai mangé __ gâteau. (I ate some cake.)

ANSWERS:

Exercise 2.1

1/ Le 2/ L' 3/ l' 4/ Les 5/ La

Exercise 2.2

1/ un 2/ une 3/ des 4/ des 5/ un

Exercise 2.3

1/ un 2/ une 3/ des 4/ la 5/ le 6/ les

Exercise 2.4

1/ le 2/ une 3/ la ; le ; la ; une 4/ la 5/ la 6/ une 7/ la ; le 8/ la 9/ le ; la ; le 10/ une

Exercise 2.5

Track 6

1/ C'est un chien (It is a dog)   2/ C'est une fille (It is a girl)   3/ Ce sont des livres (Those are books)   4/ C'est la maison de Sophie (This is the house of Sophie)   5/ C'est le livre de Jean (It is the book of Jean) 6/ Ce sont les chocolats de Patrick (Those are the chocolates of Patrick)

Exercise 2.6

Articles définis	Articles indéfinis	Articles partitifs
le, la, les	un, une, des	du, de la, des

Exercise 2.7

1/ la 2/ un 3/du 4/ des 5/ les

Exercise 2.8

1/ une 2/ un 3/ un 4/ les 5/ des

Exercise 2.9

1/ du 2/ le 3/ la 4/ de l' 5/ du

Day 3: Le verbe "être". The verb "to be".

LESSON 3: The verb être in the present tense

..and how this word seems to be popping up everywhere.

One of the most common French verbs you'll be hearing – and using – is être. It means *to be*, and will almost certainly appear frequently in daily speeches, expressions, forming other tenses, and indeed, almost everywhere else. In short, you must learn it and make it part of your basic arsenal of French words.

But there's a teeny-tiny bit of bad news: être is an *irregular verb*, which basically means **it's got rules of its own and there's no predicting the form it's going to take**. The best thing to do is to memorize the rules.

The good news? We're handing it down to you in spoonfuls. This time, let's take a look at the present tense forms of être first.

- If the pronoun being used is **je** for first person singular, you use **suis**. This means '*I am*'.
- If the pronoun is **tu** for second person singular, you use **es**. This means '*you are*'.
- For third person singular pronoun **il** or **elle**, you use **est**. This means '*he/she is*'.
- For first person plural pronoun **nous**, you use **sommes**. This means '*we are*'.
- For second person plural pronoun **vous**, you use êtes. This means '*you are*'.
- For third person plural ils or **elles**, you use the form **sont**. This means '*they are*'.

A few examples when used.

Track 7

Je **suis** heureux.- I am happy.

Tu **es** heureux.- You are happy.

Il **est** heureux.- He is happy.

Nous **sommes** heureux. - We are happy.

Vous êtes heureux. - You are happy.

Ils **sont** heureux. - They are happy.

See? It's quite easy.

Here's a little chart for guidance, if you're into that kind of thing…

Track 8

Pronoun	être form in Present Tense
Je	suis
Tu	es
il/ elle	est
Nous	sommes
Vous	êtes
ils / elles	sont

LET'S PRACTICE (aka exercises):

Exercise 3.1 - Choose the right tense of the verb *être* here.

1- Je ___ Français (I am French.)

2- Vous ___ gentil (You are nice.)

3- Désolé nous ___ en retard (Sorry, we are late.)

4- Tu ___ grand (You are tall.)

5- Ils ___ énervés (They are upset.)

6- Nous ___ contents (We are happy.)

> **Fun fact:** *French toast and french fries aren't French in origin.*

Exercise 3.2 - Tick the correct answer:

1- Je __ Français. (I am French.)

  a. est   b. sommes   c. suis

2- Ils __ mariés. (They are married.)

  a. sont   b. est   c. sommes

3- Nous __ contents. (We are happy.)

   a. sont   b. sommes   c. êtes

4- Vous __ toujours en retard. (You are always late.)

   a. êtes   b. sommes   c. sont

5- Tu __ très gentil. (You are very nice.)

   a. est   b. es   c. êtes

Exercise 3.3 - Re-order these words to make sentences that make sense:

1- suis/Je/content (am/I/happy)

2- belle/es/Tu (pretty/are/You)

3- Elle/méchante/est (she/mean/is)

4- Nous/sommes/désolés (We/are/sorry)

5- sont/à l'école/ Ils (are/at school/They)

Exercise 3.4 - Conjugate the verb « être » in the present tense:

1- Il __ un gentil garcon. (He is a nice kid.)

2- Nous __ fiers de toi. (We are proud of you.)

3- Vous __ beaux ensemble. (You are beautiful together.)

4- Elles __ soeurs. (They are sisters.)

5- je __ ravi de vous connaître. (I am delighted to meet you.)

Exercise 3.5 - Complete this dialogue with the right form of the verb « être »:

Paul : Bonjour, est-ce que Marie __ là? (Hello, is Marie here?)

La maman de Marie : Non, elle n'__ pas là. Elle __ chez le docteur avec son papa. Ils __ tous les deux malades. Tu veux lui laisser un message? Tu __ ? (No, she's not here. She went to the doctor with her dad. They are both sick. Do you want to leave a message for her? You are __?

Paul : Paul. Je __ Paul. Oui, merci beaucoup. (Paul. I am Paul. Yes, thank you very much)

Exercise 3.6 - Translate these sentences from English to French:

1- I am French.

2- He is tall.

3- They are happy. (m.)

4- We are late.

5- You are nice. (pl.)

Exercise 3.7 - Conjugate the verb « être » in the present tense:

1- Les enfants de ma sœur __ gentils. (My sister's kids are nice.)

2- Les bananes __ mûres. (The bananas are ripe.)

3- Le dîner __ délicieux. (The dinner is delicious.)

4- Moi et ma famille __ en vacances. (Me and my family are on vacation.)

5- Mes vêtements __ sales. (My clothes are dirty.)

Exercise 3.8 - Translate these sentences from French to English:

1- Ils sont Français.

2- Elle est grande.

3- Je suis content.

4- Tu es en retard.

5- Elles sont gentilles.

Exercise 3.9 - Find the mistake in each sentence and re-write it correctly:

1- Ils est Français.

2- Nous sont contents.

3- Elle sont gentille.

4- Vous es drôles. (drôles = funny)

5- Tu est en retard.

ANSWERS:

Exercise 3.1

Track 9

1/ Je suis Français (I am French.) 2/ Vous êtes gentil (You are nice.) 3/ Désolé nous sommes en retard (Sorry we are late.) 4/ Tu es grand (You are tall.) 5/ Ils sont énervés (They are upset.) 6/ Nous sommes contents (We are happy.)

Exercise 3.2

1/ suis 2/ sont 3/ sommes 4/ **êtes** 5/es

Exercise 3.3

1/ Je suis content. **2/** Tu es belle. **3/** Elle est méchante. **4/** Nous sommes désolés. **5/** Ils sont à l'école.

Exercise 3.4

1/ Il est un gentil garcon. 2/ Nous sommes fiers de toi. 3/ Vous êtes beaux ensemble. 4/ Elles sont sœurs. 5/ Je suis ravi de vous connaître.

Exercise 3.5

Paul : Bonjour, est-ce que Marie est là?

La maman de Marie : Non, elle n'est pas là. Elle est chez le docteur avec son papa. Ils sont tous les deux malades. Tu veux lui laisser un message. Tu es... ?

Paul : Paul. Je suis Paul. Oui, merci beaucoup.

Exercise 3.6

1/ Je suis Français. 2/ Il est grand. 3/ Ils sont contents. 4/ Nous sommes en retard. 5/ Vous êtes gentils.

Exercise 3.7

1/ Les enfants de ma sœur sont gentils. 2/ Les bananes sont mûres. 3/ Le dîner est délicieux. 4/ Moi et ma famille sommes en vacances. 5/ Mes vêtements sont sales.

Exercise 3.8

1/ They are French. 2/ She is tall. 3/ I am happy. 4/ You are late. 5/ They are nice.

Exercise 3.9

1/ Ils sont Français. 2/ Nous sommes contents. 3/ Elle est gentille. 4/ Vous êtes drôles. 5/ Tu est en retard.

Day 4: La négation. The negation.

LESSON 4: French Negation

...or when no can do.

Negative sentences are quite easy to make. In English, we simply pepper our words with 'not' or the shortened form "n't". In French, two words are needed to do this: **ne... pas**. Other words such as **jamais** or **rien** (nothing) can also take the place of **pas** in other instances.

Here are the French negatives.

Track 10

ne	... pas	not
ne...	rien	nothing, not...anything
ne...	personne	no one, nobody, not...anyone, not...anybody
ne...	jamais	never, not...ever
ne...	plus	no more, no longer, not...any longer, not ... anymore

Now for some basics you should take note of:

- When forming negative sentences, the verb is sandwiched in the middle of **ne** and **pas**. For example: Je **ne** parle **pas** français. (I don't speak French.) Take note that the verb **parle** is right smack in the middle of the two.

- If the verb being used starts with a vowel, **ne** is shortened to **n'**. For example: Je **n'**aime **pas** les frites. (I don't like fries.)

- When the sentence contains an object pronoun (these are 'him', 'her', or 'it' in English or te, **le**, or **lui** in French), the format changes slightly, and the object pronoun gets included in the middle of the **ne...pas** sandwich. Here's how it goes: **subject + ne + pronoun + verb + pas**. For example: Je **ne** t'entends **pas**. (I can't hear you.) where tu is shortened to t'.

- If the tense you are using contains two verbs such as the perfect tense or pluperfect, this is the format: **ne (n') + avoir or être + pas + past participle**. For example: je **n'**ai **rien** dit. (I did not say anything.)

- **Non plus** is similar to the English term 'neither'. For example: moi **non plus**. (me neither)
- In informal conversations, French speakers no longer include **ne** and just jump right in with the rest of the words. For example: Il me l'a pas dit. (He did not tell me.)

Non and **pas** are used to answer a question negatively. **Non** can mean no or not, while **pas** is used in a more emphatic way. For example: Pas moi! (Not me!) or pas question! (No way!)

LET'S PRACTICE!

Exercise 4.1 - Choose the right answer:

1. He doesn't have a laptop.
    a. Il n'a plus d'ordinateur portable.
    b. Il n'a pas d'ordinateu portable.
    c. Il n'a jamais d'ordinateu portable.
2. They didn't sing. Me neither.
    a. Elles n'ont pas chanté. Moi, non plus.
    b. Elles n'ont rien chanté. Moi, non plus.
    c. Elles n'ont plus chanté. Moi, non plus.
3. I don't want to go (there).
    a. Je ne veux jamais y aller.
    b. Je ne veux jamais plus y aller.
    c. Je ne veux pas y aller.
4. We aren't ever going.
    a. On n'a qu'à y aller.
    b. On n'y va.
    b. On n'y va jamais.
5. You aren't in New York anymore.
    a. Je ne suis plus à New York
    b. Tu n'es plus à New York.
    b. Tu n'es pas à New York.

6. We won't see it ever anymore.

    a. On ne le verra plus jamais.

    b. On ne le verra jamais.

    b. On ne le verra plus.

7. We have nothing to lose.

    a. On n'a qu'à perdre.

    b. On a tout à perdre.

    c. On n'a rien à perdre.

8. We have nothing to lose anymore.

    a. On n'a plus rien à perdre.

    b. On a plus à perdre.

    b. On n'a rien à perdre.

9. You aren't kind.

    a. Vous n'êtes ni intelligent ni gentil.

    b. Vous n'êtes jamais gentil.

    b. Vous n'êtes pas gentil.

10. We haven't seen anybody.

    a. Nous n'avons plus vu personne.

    b. Nous avons vu une personne.

    b. Nous n'avons vu personne.

Fun fact: *It's against the law to take pictures of police officers and police vehicles.*

Exercise 4.2 - Choose the right translation for each sentence:

1- I don't like cheese.

    a. Je n'aime pas le fromage.

    b. Je n'aime plus le fromage.

    c. Je n'ai jamais aimé le fromage.

2- I have never been to Japan.

    a. Je ne suis pas allé au Japon.

    b. Je ne suis jamais allé au Japon.

    c. Je voudrais aller au Japon.

3- We have nothing to lose.

    a. On n'a rien à perdre.

    b. On a tout à perdre.

    c. On n'a jamais perdu.

4- I don't like you anymore.

    a. Je ne t'aime pas.

    b. Je ne t'ai jamais aimé.

    c. Je ne t'aime plus.

5- I don't see anyone.

    a. Je ne vois personne.

    b. Je ne vois pas une personne.

    c. Je ne vois plus de personne.

Exercise 4.3 - Transform these affirmative sentences to negative ones:

1- J'aime les pommes. (I like apples.)

2- Il fait du sport. (He plays sports.)

3- Ils sont mariés. (They are married.)

4- La robe est rouge. (The dress is red.)

5- Elle travaille ici. (She works here.)

Exercise 4.4 - Transform these negative sentences to affirmative ones:

1- Cette jupe n'est pas verte. (This skirt is not green.)

2- Ce film n'est pas mauvais. (This movie is not bad.)

3- Ils ne sont pas méchants. (They are not mean.)

4- Ce travail n'est pas difficile. (This work is not hard.)

5- Je ne suis pas fatigué. (I am not tired.)

Exercise 4.5 - Choose the right translation for these sentences:

1- Il n'a jamais conduit.

    a. He always drove.

    b. He never drove.

    c. He doesn't drive.

2- Elle ne travaille plus.

   a. She's always working.

   b. She doesn't work.

   c. She doesn't work anymore.

3- Je ne connais personne ici.

   a. I know everybody here.

   b. I don't know anybody here.

   c. I don't know anymore.

4- Je n'ai pas assez d'argent pour acheter une maison.

   a. I don't have enough money to buy a house.

   b. I have enough money to buy a house.

   c. I don't have enough money to buy a house anymore.

5- Je n'ai rien à te donner.

   a. I have nothing to give you.

   b. I have nothing to give you anymore.

   c. I have something to give you.

Exercise 4.6 - Transform these affirmative sentences to negative ones:

1- Je t'aime toujours. (I still love you.)

2- La maison est grande. (The house is big.)

3- La fenêtre est ouverte. (The window is open.)

4- Je comprends tout. (I understand everything.)

5- Je parle Français. (I speak French.)

Exercise 4.7 - Choose the right answer:

1- « Je n'aime pas les olives » « Moi non plus. ». What does « moi non plus » mean here?

   a. Me neither.

   b. I don't.

   c. Me too.

2- Which one of these is said in an informal conversation?

   a. Je n'aime plus les fraises.

   b. J'aime pas les fraises.

   c. Je n'aime pas les fraises.

3- « Qui a cassé ce vase? » « Pas moi! ». What does « pas moi » mean here?

   a. Me!

   b. Not me!

   c. Him!

4- « Maman, est ce que je peux sortir ce soir ? » « Pas question! ». What does « pas question » mean here ?

   a. No way!

   b. Don't!

   c. No question!

Exercise 4.8 - Transform these affirmative sentences to negative ones:

1- Je t'entends. (I hear you.)

2- Il lui a donné de l'argent. (He gave him/her money.)

3- Je l'ai vu hier. (I saw him yesterday.)

4- Elle lui demande son numéro de téléphone. (She asks him for his phone number.)

5- Je lui parle en Français. (I talk to him in French.)

Exercise 4.9 - Complete these sentences with « pas », « plus », « rien », « personne » ou « jamais » :

1- J'aimais ce film avant. Maintenant, je ne l'aime ____. (I liked this movie before. Now, I don't like it anymore.)

2- J'aimerais bien voyager. Je ne l'ai __ fait. (I would like to travel. I've never done it.)

3- Je n'ai __ fait de toute la journée. (I've done nothing all day long.)

4- Où sont les gens ? Je ne vois __ ici. (Where are the people? I don't see anyone here.)

5- Hier, j'ai fait la vaisselle. Aujourd'hui, je ne l'ai __. (Yesterday, I washed the dishes. Today, I didn't do it.)

ANSWERS:

Exercise 4.1

Track 11

1/ B. Il n'a pas d'ordinateur portable. 2/ A. Elles n'ont pas chanté. Moi, non plus. 3/ C. Je ne veux pas y aller. 4/ C. On n'y va jamais. 5/ B. Tu n'es plus à New York. 6/ A. On ne le verra plus jamais. 7/ C. On n'a rien à perdre. 8/ A. On n'a plus rien à perdre. 9/ C. Vous n'êtes pas gentil. 10/ C. Nous n'avons vu personne

Exercise 4.2

1/ Je n'aime pas le fromage. 2/ Je ne suis jamais allé au Japon. 3/ On n'a rien à perdre. 4/ Je ne t'aime plus. 5/ Je ne vois personne.

Exercise 4.3

1/ Je n'aime pas les pommes. 2/ Il ne fait pas du sport. 3/ Ils ne sont pas mariés. 4/ La robe n'est pas rouge. 5/ Elle ne travaille pas ici.

Exercise 4.4

1/ Cette jupe est verte. 2/ Ce film est mauvais. 3/ Ils sont méchants. 4/ Ce travail est difficile. 5/ Je suis fatigué.

Exercise 4.5

1/ He never drove. 2/ She doesn't work anymore. 3/ I don't know anybody here. 4/ I don't have enough money to buy a house. 5/ I have nothing to give you.

Exercise 4.6

1/ Je ne t'aime plus. 2/ La maison n'est pas grande. 3/ La fenêtre n'est pas ouverte. 4/ Je ne comprends rien. 5/ Je ne parle pas Français.

Exercise 4.7

1/ Me neither. 2/ J'aime pas les fraises. 3/ not me 4/ No way!

Exercise 4.8

1/ Je ne t'entends pas. 2/ Il ne lui a pas donné de l'argent. 3/ Je ne l'ai pas vu hier. 4/ Elle ne lui demande pas son numéro de téléphone. 5/ Je ne lui parle pas en Français.

Exercise 4.9

1/ plus 2/ jamais 3/ rien 4/ personne 5/ pas

Day 5: Il y a. There is.

LESSON 5: The French Expression 'Il y a'

...there is a...bunch of uses for this.

One of the most common expressions you'll come across in French is **il y a** which means 'there is a' or 'there are'.

Pronounced as 'ee lya', it can appear in basic statements, questions, negative sentences, and other tenses. In short, you'll find that it is basically all over the place.

Using **il y a** is a quick and easy way to say a lot of things in a simple format. This is why you should take this time to familiarize yourself with its different permutations and uses.

Here are some important things to remember about il y a.

- Il y a is composed of these three words: **il** (which more or less means it in English), **y**

(meaning, there), and **a**, the third person singular form of the verb avoir which means to have. Its literal translation means *'it has there'*.

- It usually follows these patterns:

  (1) il y a + indefinite article + noun, (2) il y a + number + noun,

  (3) il y a + indefinite pronoun. For example: Il y a un chien. (There is a dog.)

- It can be used with both singular and plural nouns. Just like this: **Il y a deux chiens**. *(There are two dogs.)*

- It can be used to ask a question using the est-ce que format. **Est-ce qu'il y a un chien?** *(Is there a dog?)*

- It can also be used to ask a question using inversion. Such as this: **Y a-t-il un chien?** *(Is there a dog?)*

- You can use question words with it too! **Pourquoi est-ce qu'il y a un chien?** *(Why is there a dog?)*

- It could appear in this format too: **Qu'est-ce qu'il y a?** This can be loosely translated to *"What is it?"*
- When you want to use it in a negative sentence, you simply change it to il n'y a pas and change the indefinite article to de. For example: **Il n'y a pas de chien.** *(There is no dog.)*
- If you want to use il y a in a different tense, you need to conjugate the verb avoir to match the tense you are going to use. Some examples: **Il y avait un chien.** *(There was a dog.)* **Il y aura des chiens.** *(There will be some dogs).*

LET'S PRACTICE!

Exercise 5.1 - Answer this question by using "il y a"

1. - Dans la cuisine, il y a un four ?

2. - Dans votre salon, il y a une table et un canapé ?

3. - Dans votre chambre, il y a un grand lit ou un petit lit?

4. - Dans la salle de bains, il y a une douche ou une baignoire?

Form some sentences similar with the example below

E.g: Chine / Panda. En Chine, il y a des pandas.

1. Japon / Girafes _____

   _____

2. Paris/ Tour Eiffel _____

   _____

3. Londres / la Statue de la Liberté (Statue of the Liberty) _____

   _____

4. Australie / kangourous _____

   _____

Fun fact: *The French had an early version of the internet called Minitel as long ago as 1984, they could pay bills and shop at home using the Minitel service.*

Exercise 5.2

Create sentences similar to the example below:

Example: Fleurs/Jardin. ➔ Dans le jardin, il y a des fleurs. (In the garden, there are flowers.)

1- Nuages/Ciel. (clouds/sky)

2- Élèves/École. (pupils/school)

3- Jouets/Chambre de l'enfant. (toys/kid's room)

4- Tables/Salle de classe. (Tables/Classroom)

5- Vêtements/Machine à laver. (Clothes/Washing machine)

Exercise 5.3 - Transform these affirmative sentences to negative ones:

Example: Il y a un chien. (There is a dog) ➔ Il n'y a pas de chien. (There is no dog.)

1- Il y a un miroir dans le salon. (There is a mirror in the living room.)

2- Il y a du lait dans le réfrigérateur. (There is milk in the fridge.)

3- Il y a des oiseaux dans le ciel. (There are birds in the sky.)

4- Il y a des voitures dans le parking. (There are cars in the parking lot.)

5- Il y a un crayon dans ma trousse. (There is a pencil in my pencil case.)

Exercise 5.4 - Create questions using the est-ce que format (see the example below):

Example: Un chien/Jardin. ➔ Est ce qu'il y a un chien dans le jardin ? (Is there a dog in the garden ?)

1- Une chambre libre/hôtel. (a free room/hotel)

2- Du sucre/Café. (sugar/coffee)

3- Des cours de danse/Salle de gym. (dance classes/gym)

4- Un lion/Zoo. (a lion/zoo)

5- Des toilettes/ici. (toilets/here)

Exercise 5.5 - Create questions using inversions (see the example below):

Example: Il y a un chien. ➔ Y a-t-il un chien ? (Is there a dog ?)

1- Il y a un concert. (There is a concert.)

2- Il y a un climatiseur dans la chambre. (There is an air conditioner in the room.)

3- Il y a un balcon dans cet appartement. (There is a balcony in this apartment.)

4- Il y a une banque près d'ici. (There is a bank near here.)

5- Il y a des taxis par ici. (There are taxis here.)

ANSWERS:

Exercise 5.1

Track 12

Answer to this question by using "il y a"

1/ Oui dans la cuisine il y a un four. 2/ Oui il y a une table et un canapé. 3/ Il y a un petit lit 4/ Il y a une douche

Form some similar sentences with the examples below.

1/ Il n'y a pas de girafe au Japon. 2/ Il y a la tour Eiffel à Paris. 3/ Il n'y a pas la Statue de la Liberté à Londres 4. En Australie; Il y a des Kangourous.

Exercise 5.2

1/ Dans le ciel, il y a des nuages. 2/ Dans l'école, i y a des élèves. 3/ Dans la chambre de l'enfant, il y a des jouets. 4/ Dans la salle de classe, il y a des tables. 5/ Dans la machine à laver, il y a des vêtements.

Exercise 5.3

1/ Il n'y a pas de miroir dans le salon. 2/ Il n'y a pas de l'air dans le réfrigérateur. 3/ Il n'y a pas d'oiseau dans le ciel. 4/ Il n'y a pas de voiture dans le parking. 5/ Il n'y a pas de crayon dans ma trousse.

Exercise 5.4

1/ Est ce qu'il y a une chambre libre dans l'hôtel ? 2/ Est-ce qu'il y a du sucre dans le café ? 3/ Est-ce qu'il y a des cours de danse dans la salle de gym ? 4/ Est-ce qu'il y a un lion dans le zoo ? 5/ Est-ce qu'il y a des toilettes ici ?

Exercise 5.5

1/ Y a-t-il un concert? 2/ Y a-t-il un climatiseur dans la chambre? 3/ Y a-t-il un balcon dans cet appartement? 4/ Y a-t-il une banque près d'ici? 5/ Y a-t-il des taxis près d'ici?

Day 6: Poser des questions. Asking questions.

LESSON 6: 5 Ways to Ask Questions

There are not one, not two, but five different ways to ask questions in French. From the very simple to the downright complicated, you may take your pick. But before you get the opportunity, you should be familiar with all of them first.

1. TURNING A STATEMENT INTO A QUESTION

This is by far the easiest because all you have to do is simply use any statement and make it a question by changing the pitch of your voice. In writing, just add a question mark at the end and you're all set.

Take these examples:

Track 13

C'est vrai. (That's true.)

C'est vrai? (Is that true?)

Vous aimez la France. (You like France.)

Vous aimez la France? (Do you like France?)

2. USING EST-CE QUE

Another way is to add **est-ce que** to the beginning of a sentence. **Est-ce que** literally means "is it that" in English, and inserting it before a regular statement can turn it into a question. The rest of the sentence structure stays the same. Easy enough?

Track 14

For example: **Est-ce qu'il est arrivé?** (Has he arrived?)

Exercise 6.1 - Change these statements into questions using « est-ce que » :

1- Vous aimez la France. (You like France.)

2- C'est votre chien. (It's your dog.)

3- Vous parlez le Français. (You talk French.)

4- Il est un bon ami. (He's a good friend.)

5- Elle est arrivée. (She arrived.)

3. CHANGING THE ORDER OF THE WORDS TO FORM A QUESTION (INVERSION)

This is the formal way of asking questions in French, and all you need to do is move the sentence structure around a bit. Normally, the subject is followed by the verb, but for the inverted questions, the verb is placed before the subject and then joined by a hyphen.

Example:

Track 15

Vous aimez la France. (You like France.)

Aimez-vous la France? (Do you like France?)

Exercise 6.2 - Change these statements into questions using « est-ce que » :

1- Vous aimez la France. (You like France.)

2- C'est votre chien. (It's your dog.)

3- Vous parlez le Français. (You talk French.)

4- Il est un bon ami. (He's a good friend.)

5- Elle est arrivée. (She arrived.)

4. USING N'EST-CE PAS PAS OR NON

If you're confident that the person you are talking to agrees with you, you can add n'est-ce pas at the end of the sentence. It is just similar to the English usage of "isn't it?" or "right?" at the end of a question.

Non works the same way. It literally means "no" and is also added at the end of the sentence. Another one is **hein**. It is just like saying "eh?" in English, and is often used in informal conversation.

Some examples:

Track 16

Vous aimez la France, n'est-ce pas?	You like France, don't you?
Il est arrivé, n'est-ce pas?	He arrived, didn't he?
Vous aimez la France, non?	You like France, right?
Vous aimez la France, hein?	You like France, eh?

Exercise 6.3 - Change these statements into questions using « n'est-ce pas » or « non » :

1- Il fait du sport. (He plays sports.)

2- Elle est à la maison. (She's at home.)

3- Tu as lavé la vaisselle. (You cleaned the dishes.)

4- Tu aimes le vin. (You like wine.)

5- Ils sont ensemble. (They are together.)

5. USING QUESTION WORDS

Last, but definitely not the easiest, is to use interrogative words. The question words may be placed at the start or end of the sentence. It can also appear right before est-ce que, or before the inverted subject and verb.

Example: **When did you arrive?**

Track 17

Quand est-ce que tu es arrivé?
Quand es-tu arrivé?
Quand t'es arrivé?
T'es arrivé quand?

The commonly used question words:

combien + verb?	how much?, how many?
combien de + noun?	how much?, how many?
comment?	how?
où?	where?
pourquoi?	why?
quand?	when?
qui? que? and quoi	Who, whom, or what (depending on the usage)
quel, quels, quelle, or quelles?	Who, which, or what (depending on how it's used)
lequel? laquelle? lesquels? and lesquelles?	Which one? (this is the different forms of lequel based on gender and count)

Exercise 6.4 - Complete these questions with the right question words:

1- ___ coûte ce téléphone? (___costs this phone.)

2- ___ frères et soeurs avez-vous? (___ brothers and sisters have you?)

3- ___ sont mes nouvelles chaussures ? (___ are my new shoes ?)

4- ___ faire pour aller à la gare ? (___ to do to go to the train station ?)

5- ___ aimes-tu les chiens? (__ do you like dogs?)

Exercise 6.5 - Complete these questions with the right question words:

1- ___ les cours commencent-ils? (___ do classes begin ?)

2- ___ d'entre vous est médecin? (___of you is a doctor?)

3- ___ est le président de la France? (___ is the president of France ?)

4- ___ est ton film préféré? (___ is your favourite movie?)

5- ___ veut dire « salut » en Français ? (__ does « salut » mean in French ?)

LET'S PRACTICE SOME MORE!

Exercise 6.6 - Fill in the blanks with the correct answer:

1. (Elle aide) ___ Corinne à faire ses devoirs? Does she help Corinne with her homework?

Aide-elle?   Aide-t elle?   Aide t-elle?   Aide-t-elle?

2. (Vois-tu) _____ Paul? Can you see Paul?

Est ce que tu vois? Est-ce que tu vois? Estce que tu vois? Est-que tu vois?

3. (Que fait-il) _____ ce week-end? What's he doing this weekend?

Q'est-ce qu'il fait? Qu'est-ce qu'il fait? Qu'estce-qu'il fait? Quesqu'il fait?

4. (What) ___ veux-tu pour Noël? What do you want for Christmas?

Que? Quand? Qu'? Qui?

5. (Vous avez écouté) _____la radio hier soir? Did you listen to the radio last night?

Avez-vous-écouté? Avez vous écouté? Avezvous écouté? Vous-avez écouté?

6. (Aime-t-elle) _____ les chats? Does she like cats?

Est-ce-qu'elle aime? Est ce qu'elle aime? Estc'est elle aime? Est-ce qu'elle aime?

7. (Who) ___ as-tu rencontré au supermarché? Who did you meet in the supermarket?

Quand? Qu'? Que? Qui?

8. (Vous étudiez) _____ l'anglais depuis longtemps? Have you been learning English for a long time?

Etudiez-vous? Vous étudiez-vous? Etudiez-tvous? Etudiez vous?

9. (Vont-ils) _____ en France cette année? Are they going to France this year?

Est ce qu'ils vont? Est-qu'ils vont? Est-ce qu'ils vont? Est-ce-qu'ils vont?

10. (Tu sais) _____ jouer de la guitare? Can you play the guitar?

Tu-sais? Tu sais? Sais-tu? Sais tu?

Fun fact: *It's illegal to kiss on railways in France (oops).*

Exercise 6.7 - Choose the correct answer:

1- You want to ask somebody his/her name, you should say:

    a. Comment t'appelles tu? (informal)/ Comment vous appelez-vous? (formal)

    b. Qui es-tu ? (informal)/ Qui êtes-vous? (formal)

    c. Qui t'appelles tu ? (informal)/ qui vous appelez-vous? (formal)

2- You want to ask somebody his/her age, you should say:

    a. Quand est ton âge? / Quand est votre âge?

    b. Quel âge as-tu ?/ Quel âge avez-vous?

    c. Combien est ton âge? / Combien est votre âge?

3- You want to know where the toilets are, you should say:

    a. Y a-t-il des toilettes?

    b. Où sont les toilettes ?

    c. Combien y a-t-il de toilettes?

4- You want to know when the train arrives, you should say:

    a. Où est le train?

    b. Quel est le train pour Paris?

    c. Quand est ce que le train arrive?

Exercise 6.8 - Choose the correct translation:

1- What are you doing this weekend?

    a. Que fait-il ce week-end?

    b. Que fais-tu ce week-end ?

    c. Quand est le week-end ?

2- When are you coming ?

    a. D'où est-ce que vous venez ?

    b. Quand venez-vous?

    c. Comment venez-vous ?

3- Where do you live?

    a. Où est ce que vous habitez?

    b. Qui habite avec vous?

    c. Pourquoi habitez-vous ici?

4- Do you have a brother or a sister?

    a. Combien as-tu de frères et sœurs?

    b. As-tu un frère ou une sœur?

    c. Où sont tes frères et sœurs?

5- Which one of them is your dog?

    a. Où est ton chien?

    b. Comment va ton chien?

    c. Lequel d'entre eux est ton chien?

Exercise 6.9 - Choose the correct translation:

1- Do you like cats?

    a. Quel chat aimes-tu?

    b. Pourquoi aimes-tu les chats?

    c. Aimes-tu les chats?

2- Where is he?

    a. Où est-il?

    b. Quand est ce qu'il arrive?

    c. Qui est-il?

3- Did you eat lunch today?

    a. Avez-vous déjeuné aujourd'hui?

    b. Voudrais-tu déjeuner aujourd'hui?

    c. Quand est-ce que tu as déjeuné aujourd'hui?

4- Who sings this song?

    a. Qui chante cette chanson?

    b. Qui chantait cette chanson?

    c. Où se chante cette chanson?

5- Which one of you is Marie?

    a. Lequel d'entre vous est Marie?

    b. Laquelle d'entre vous est Marie?

    c. Qui est Marie?

ANSWERS:

Exercice 6.1

1/ Est-ce que vous aimez la France? 2/ Est-ce que c'est votre chien? 3/ Est-ce que vous parlez le Français? 4/ Est-ce qu'il est un bon ami? 5/ Est-ce qu'elle est arrivée ?

Exercice 6.2

1/ Est-ce que vous aimez la France? 2/ Est-ce que c'est votre chien? 3/ Est-ce que vous parlez le Français? 4/ Est-ce qu'il est un bon ami? 5/ Est-ce qu'elle est arrivée?

Exercice 6.3

1/ Il fait du sport, n'est-ce pas? 2/ Elle est à la maison, non? 3/ Tu as lavé la vaisselle, n'est-ce pas? 4/ Tu aimes le vin, n'est-ce pas? 5/ Ils sont ensemble, non?

Exercice 6.4

1/ Combien coûte ce téléphone? 2/ Combien de frères et sœurs avez-vous? 3/ Où sont mes nouvelles chaussures? 4/ Comment faire pour aller à la gare? 5/ Pourquoi aimes-tu les chiens?

Exercice 6.5

1/ Quand les cours commencent-ils? 2/ Lequel d'entre vous est médecin? 3/ Qui est le président de la France? 4/ Quel est ton film préféré? 5/ Que veut dire « salut » en Français?

Exercice 6.6

Track 18

1/ Aide-t elle Corinne à faire ses devoirs? 2/ Est-ce que tu vois? Paul? 3/ Qu'est-ce qu'il fait ce week-end? 4/ Que veux-tu pour Noël? 5/ Avez-vous écouté la radio hier soir? 6/ Est-ce-qu'elle aime les chats? 7/ Qui as-tu rencontré au supermarché? 8/ Etudiez-vous l'anglais depuis longtemps? 9/ Est-ce qu'ils vont en France cette année? 10/ Sais-tu jouer de la guitare?

Exercise 6.7

1/ Comment t'appelles tu? (informal)/ Comment vous appelez-vous? (formal) 2/ Quel âge as-tu ?/ Quel âge avez-vous ? 3/ Où sont les toilettes ? 4/ Quand est ce que le train arrive ?

Exercise 6.8

1/ Que fais-tu ce week-end? 2/ Quand venez-vous? 3/ Où est ce que vous habitez? 4/ As-tu un frère ou une sœur? 5/ Lequel d'entre eux est ton chien?

Exercise 6.9

1/ Aimes-tu les chats? 2/ Où est-il? 3/ Avez-vous déjeuné aujourd'hui? 4/ Qui chante cette chanson? 5/ Laquelle d'entre vous est Marie?

Day 7: Le présent simple. Simple present.

LESSON 7: French Simple Present

When we talk about a current action, something that is true in the moment, habitual events, or widely accepted truths, we use the simple present tense.

Regular verbs fall into either of these three categories: those that end in -er, -ir, and -re. To conjugate these verbs, you have to take note of the applicable rules for each type.

Ready? Let's start with the -er verbs.

- To form the present tense for the -er verbs, use the infinitive, chop off the -er and add the new ending which depends on the subject of the sentence. For example, the verb donner is changed to its stem donn + the new ending.

Track 19

- For first-person singular, add the new ending -e. **Je donne.** (I give)
- For second-person singular, add -es. **Tu donnes** (You give)
- For third-person singular, add -e. **Il/Elle donne** (He/she gives)
- For first-person plural, add -ons. **Nous donnons** (We give)
- For second-person plural, add -ez. **Vous donnez** (You give)
- •For third-person plural, add -ent. **Ils/elles donnent** (They give)

Exercise 7.1 - Conjugate the verbs between brackets in the simple present tense:

1- Je (aimer) ____ énormément ce film. (I really like this movie.)

2- Ils (travailler) ____ jour et nuit. (They work day and night.)

3- Elle (parler) ____ très bien le Français. (She speaks French very well.)

4- Nous (manger) ____ dehors ce soir. (We eat out tonight.)

5- Vous (payer) ____ en espèces ou par carte de crédit? (Are you going to pay in cash or by credit card?)

Now for the -ir verbs.

- To form the present tense for the -ir verbs, use the infinitive, chop off the -ir and add the new ending. For example, the verb finir is changed to its stem fin + the new ending.

Track 20

- For first-person singular, add -is. **Je finis** (I finish)
- For second-person singular, add -is. **Tu finis** (You finish)
- For third-person singular, add -it. **Il/Elle finit** (He/she finishes)
- For first-person plural, add -issons. **Nous finissons** (We finish)
- For second-person plural, add -issez. **Vous finissez** (You finish)
- For third-person plural, add -issent. **Ils/elles finissent** (They finish)

Finally, for the -re verbs

Track 21

To form the present tense for the -re verbs, use the infinitive, chop off the -re and add the new ending. For example, the verb prendre is changed to its stem attend + the new ending.

- For first-person singular, add -s. **Je prends** (I take)
- For second-person singular, add -s. **Tu prends** (You take)
- For third-person singular, don't add anything. **Il/Elle prend** (He/she takes)
- For first-person plural, add -ons. **Nous prenons** (We take)
- For second-person plural, add -ez. **Vous prenez** (You take)
- For third-person plural, add -ent. **Ils/Elles prennent** (They take)

Track 22

Another example

- For first-person singular, add -s. **J'attends** (I wait)
- For second-person singular, add -s. **Tu attends** (You wait)
- For third-person singular, don't add anything. **Il/Elle attend** (He/she waits)
- For first-person plural, add -ons. **Nous attendons** (We wait)
- For second-person plural, add -ez. **Vous attendez** (You wait)
- For third-person plural, add -ent. **Ils/Elles attendent** (They wait)

LET'S PRACTICE!

Exercise 7.2 - Fill in the blanks with the correct answer:

1. Il (écouter) _____ beaucoup la radio. (He listens to the radio a lot.)

2. Nous (aimer) _____ ce film. (We like this film.)

3. Elle (travailler) _____ à Paris. (She works in Paris.)

4. Les enfants (grandir) _____ très vite. (The children are growing up fast.

5. Il (vendre) ____ sa voiture. (He's selling his car.)

6. Elle (parler) _____ couramment le français. (She speaks French fluently.)

7. Nous ne (vendre) _____ pas de chaussures. (We don't sell shoes.)

8. Tu ne (répondre) _____ pas à ma question. (You're not answering my question.)

> **Fun fact:** *French is the official language of the United Nations.*

Exercise 7.3 - Change the following sentences into plural:

1- Il mange du gâteau. (He eats cake.)

2- J'adore la musique. (I adore music.)

3- Tu danses très bien. (You dance very well.)

4- Elle joue aux cartes. (She plays cards.)

5- Je cherche les toilettes. (I'm looking for the toilets.)

Exercise 7.4 - Conjugate the verbs between brackets in the simple present tense:

1- Elle (finir) ___ ses devoirs avant de jouer. (She finishes her homework before playing.)

2- Nous (réfléchir) ___ à une solution. (We are thinking about a solution.)

3- Je (rougir) ___ quand je le vois. (I blush when I see him.)

4- Vous (choisir) ___ quelle option? (You choose which option?)

5- Ils (applaudir) ___ quand le spectacle est fini. (They applaud when the show is over.)

Exercise 7.5 - Change the following sentences into singular:

1- Nous choisissons de partir en vacances. (We choose to go on vacation.)

2- Elles réussissent à finir l'examen à temps. (They succeed to finish the exam in time.)

3- Ils grandissent vite. (They grow up so fast.)

4- Vous réfléchissez trop. (You think a lot.)

5- Ils n'obéissent pas aux ordres. (They don't obey orders.)

Exercise 7.6 - Conjugate the verbs between brackets in the simple present tense:

1- Nous (attendre) ___ le résultat depuis ce matin. (We've been waiting for the results since this morning.)

2- Je (prendre) ___ quelle route pour aller au supermarché? (I take which road to go to the supermarket?)

3- Ils (vendre) ___ de beaux vêtements. (They sell beautiful clothes.)

4- Elle (répondre) ___ au téléphone rapidement. (She answers the phone quickly.)

5- Vous (descendre) ___ ici? (Are you coming down here?)

Exercise 7.7 - Change the following sentences from into singular, or from plural into singular:

1- J'attends depuis longtemps. (I'm waiting since a long time.)

2- Nous rendons visite à notre grand-mère. (We visit our grandmother.)

3- Il entend un bruit étrange venant de dehors. (He hears a weird sound coming from outside.)

4- Répondez aux questions. (Answer the questions.)

5- Je perds toujours mes clés. (I always lose my keys.)

Exercise 7.8 - Conjugate the verbs between brackets in the simple present tense:

1- Il (parler) ___ bien l'anglais. (He speaks English well.)

2- Elles (répondre) ___ à toutes les questions. (They answer all the questions.)

3- Nous (choisir) ___ de dormir à l'hôtel ce soir. (We choose to sleep at the hotel tonight.)

4- J'(attendre) ___ le métro. (I'm waiting for the metro.)

5- Vous (marcher) ___ assez vite. (You walk fast enough.)

ANSWERS:

Exercise 7.1

1/ J'aime énormément ce film. 2/ Ils travaillent jour et nuit. 3/ Elle parle très bien le Français. 4/ Nous mangeons dehors ce soir. 5/ Vous payez en espèces ou par carte de crédit ?

Exercise 7.2

Track 23

1/ Il écoute beaucoup la radio. 2/ Nous aimons ce film? 3/ Elle travaille à Paris. 4/ Les enfants grandissent très vite. 5/ Il vend sa voiture. 6/ Elle parle couramment le francais. 7/ Nous ne vendons pas de chaussures. 8/ Tu ne réponds pas à ma question.

Exercise 7.3

1/ Ils mangent du gâteau. 2/ Nous adorons la musique. 3/ Vous dancez très bien. 4/ Elles jouent aux cartes. 5/ Nous cherchons les toilettes.

Exercise 7.4

1/ Elle finit ses devoirs avant de jouer. 2/ Nous réfléchissons à une solution. 3/ Je rougis quand je le vois. 4/ Vous choisissez quelle option? 5/ Ils applaudissent quand le spectacle est fini.

Exercise 7.5

1/ Je choisis de partir en vacances. 2/ Elle réussit à finir l'examen à temps. 3/ Il grandit vite. 4/ Tu réfléchis trop. 5/ Il n'obéit pas aux ordres.

Exercise 7.6

1/ Nous attendons le résultat depuis ce matin. 2/ Je prends quelle route pour aller au supermarché? 3/ Ils vendent de beaux vêtements. 4/ Elle répond au téléphone. 5/ Vous descendez ici?

Exercise 7.7

1/ Nous attendons depuis longtemps. 2/ Je rends visite à ma grand-mère. 3/ Ils entendent un bruit étrange venant de dehors. 4/ Réponds aux questions. 5/ Nous perdons toujours nos clés.

Exercise 7.8

1/ Il parle bien l'anglais. 2/ Elles répondent à toutes les questions. 3/ Nous choisissons de dormir à l'hôtel ce soir. 4/ J'attends le métro. 5/ Vous marchez assez vite.

Day 8: The Quick Way to Express Past, Present, and Future

LESSON 8: The Quick Way to Express Past, Present, and Future

...or how shortcuts work.

Fancy a quick little jaunt on the express train? I know you do. So, what if I told you that you could actually skip the process and instantly learn to talk in French about

- recent past
- near future, and
- ongoing actions

Sounds awesome? Certainly is. All this will happen with the use of the **indicative form of the verb,** which is its *basic form.* The best part is, you no longer need to conjugate the verb for the action you're referring to.

1. Expressing recent past using the verb venir

Venir is an irregular verb which means *to come.* When used this way, it can be loosely translated to the English term "just". Such as, "I just ate".

- This is the format to follow: The conjugated present form of **'venir'** + **de + the infinitive form of the action that recently happened.**
- Use this table for the present forms of venir.

Track 24

Pronoun	Venir form in Present Tense	Example
Je	viens	**Je viens de manger.** (I just ate.)
Tu	viens	**Tu viens de manger.** (You just ate.)
Il	vient	**Il vient de manger.** (He just ate.)
Nous	venons	**Nous venons de manger.** (We just ate.)
Vous	venez	**Vous venez de manger.** (You just ate.)
Ils	viennent	**Ils viennent de manger.** (They just ate.)

Exercise 8.1 - Complete these sentences to express recent past using the verb "venir":

1- Je ___ (manger) une soupe. (I just ate a soup.)

2- Il ___ (sortir). (He just got out.)

3- Elle ___ (finir) ses devoirs. (She just finished her homework.)

4- Nous ___ (monter) dans le train. (We just got on the train.)

5- Ils ___ (partir) pour se reposer. (They just left to rest.)

Exercise 8.2 - Transform these sentences to express recent past using the verb "venir":

1- Je parle à mon patron. (I talk to my boss.)

2- Elle prend une douche. (She takes a shower.)

3- Ils finissent leur réunion. (They finish their meeting.)

4- Nous terminons l'examen final. (We're finishing the final exam.)

5- Le professeur explique la nouvelle leçon. (The teacher explains the new lesson.)

2. Expressing the near future using the verb aller (Futur Proche)

Another commonly used irregular French verb is the word "**aller**". While it literally means '*to go*', it is also used as a casual way of expressing the near-future tense. Its English counterpart would be saying "going to", such as "I'm going to sleep in a while."

- This is the format to follow: The conjugated present form of '**aller**' + **the infinitive form of the action that is about to happen**.

- Use this table for the present forms of aller, as well as some examples.

Track 25

Pronoun	Aller form in Present Tense	Example
Je	vais	**Je vais partir.** (I am going to leave.)
Tu	vas	**Tu vas partir.** (You are going to leave.)
Il	va	**Il va partir.** (He is going to leave.)
Nous	allons	**Nous allons partir.** (We are going to leave.)
Vous	allez	**Vous allez partir.** (You are going to leave.)
Ils	vont	**Ils vont partir.** (They are going to leave.)

Exercise 8.3 - Complete these sentences to express the near future using the verb "aller":

1- Je ___ (faire) du ski. (I am going to ski)

2- Nous ___ (jouer) au Football. (We're going to play Football)

3- Il ___ (essayer) d'écrire un livre. (He's going to try to write a book)

4- Elle ___ (raconter) une histoire aux enfants. (She's going to read a story to the kids)

5- Vous ___ (finir) votre travail un peu tard aujourd'hui. (You're going to finish your work a bit late today)

Exercise 8.4 - Transform these sentences to express the near future using the verb "aller":

1- Je visite la France. (I visit France.)

2- Je me promène dans le parc. (I walk in the park.)

3- Il pleut. (It's raining.)

4- Je prends le train pour aller à Paris. (I take the train to go to Paris.)

5- Ils participent au tournoi de golf. (They participate in the gold tournament.)

3. Expressing ongoing action using the expression être en train de

Unlike English, the French language does not have a direct counterpart of the present progressive verb form. The simple present tense is used to mean both simple present and present progressive. But when you fancy being more precise, you can always use the French expression être en train de which literally means to be _____-ing or to be in the middle of doing something.

• This is the format to follow: **The conjugated present form of ' être' + en train de + the infinitive form of the action that is about to happen.**

Here are the conjugated forms of the irregular verb être and some examples of how it works.

Track 26

Pronoun	être form in Present Tense	Examples
Je	suis	**Je suis en train de parler.** I am speaking (right now).
tu	es	**Tu es en train de parler.** You are speaking (right now).
il	est	**Il est en train de parler.** He is speaking (right now).
Nous	sommes	**Nous sommes en train de parler.** We are speaking (right now).
Vous	êtes	**Vous êtes en train de parler.** You are speaking (right now).
ils	sont	**Ils sont en train de parler.** They are speaking (right now).

Exercise 8.5 - Complete these sentences to express an ongoing action using the expression "être en train de":

1- Je ___ (boire) du chocolat chaud. (I am drinking hot chocolate.)

2- Elle ___ (appeler) sa mère au téléphone. (She's calling her mother on the phone.)

3- Nous ___ (faire) le ménage. (We are doing the household chores)

4- Ils ___ (regarder) un film. (They're watching a movie.)

5- Vous ___ (perdre) votre temps. (You are wasting your time.)

Exercise 8.6 - Transform these sentences to express an ongoing action using the expression "être en train de":

1- Je regarde un film. (I watch a movie.)

2- Je chante sous la douche. (I sing in the shower.)

3- Tu fais de ton mieux. (You do your best.)

4- Il fait de la musique dans sa chambre. (He makes music in his room.)

5- Nous faisons du shopping. (We're doing shopping.)

LET'S PRACTICE SOME MORE!

Exercise 8.7 - Find the right tense:

1. Il _____arriver au marché. He's just arrived at the market.

2. Ils ____ se marier en avril. They're going to get married in April.

3. Jack ___ être diplômé. Jack just graduated

4. Je ___étudier la chimie I am studying chemistry.

5. Je ___ rencontrer mon ami I am going to meet my friend.

> **Fun fact:** *French was the official language of England for over 300 years.*

Exercise 8.8 - Conjugate the verbs "venir", "aller" and "être" in simple present :

	Venir	Aller	être
Je			
Tu			
Il/Elle			
Nous			
Vous			
Ils/Elles			

ANSWERS:

Exercise 8.1

1/ Je viens de manger une soupe. 2/ Il vient de sortir. 3/ Elle vient de finir ses devoirs. 4/ Nous venons de monter dans le train. 5/ Ils viennent de partir pour se reposer.

Exercise 8.2

1/ Je viens de parler à mon patron. 2/ Elle vient de prendre une douche. 3/ Ils viennent de finir leur reunion 4/ Nous venons de terminer l'examen final. 5/ Le professeur vient d'expliquer la nouvelle leçon.

Exercise 8.3

1/ Je vais faire du ski. 2/ Nous allons jouer au Football. 3/ Il va essayer d'écrire un livre. 4/ Elle va raconter une histoire aux enfants. 5. Vous allez finir votre travail un peu tard aujourd'hui.

Exercise 8.4

1/ Je vais visiter la France. 2/ Je vais me promener dans le parc. 3/ Il va pleuvoir. 4/ Je vais prendre le train pour aller à Paris. 5/ Ils vont participer au tournoi de golf.

Exercise 8.5

1/ Je suis en train de boire du chocolat chaud. 2/ Elle est en train d'appeler sa mère au téléphone. 3/ Nous sommes en train de faire le ménage. 4/ Ils sont en train de regarder un film. 5/ Vous êtes en train de perdre votre temps.

Exercise 8.6

1/ Je suis en train de regarder un film. 2/ Je suis en train de chanter sous la douche. 3/ Tu es en train de faire de ton mieux. 4/ Il est en train de faire de la musique dans sa chambre. 5/ Nous sommes en train de faire du shopping.

Exercise 8.7

Track 27

1/ Il vient d'arriver au marché. 2/ Ils vont se marier en avril. 3/ Jack vient d'être diplômé. 4/ Je suis en train d'étudier la chimie. 5/ Je vais rencontrer mon ami.

Exercise 8.8

	Venir	Aller	être
Je	viens	vais	suis
Tu	viens	vas	es
Il/Elle	vient	va	est
Nous	venons	allons	sommes
Vous	venez	allez	êtes
Ils/Elles	viennent	vont	sont

Day 9: en and y

LESSON 9: "en" and "y"

... or little words that make a huge difference.

Say hello to your new adverbial pronoun friends **en** and **y**: they're two of a kind and are very important in daily conversing. **En** and **Y** have different uses, and how they are used has different translations in English.

Here are some basic rules to remember about these two.

EN

- En is used to replace verbs and phrases which use de. This is to avoid repeating the same words.

- It can mean 'some' or 'any' when it is not followed by a noun. For example: **Avez-vous des chiens?** *(Do you have any dogs?)* **Oui, nous en avons.** *(Yes, we have some.)*

- It can also mean '*of it*' or '*of them*'. For example: **Ont-ils des chiens?** *(Do they have any dogs?)* **Oui, ils ent ont deux.** *(Yes, they have two of them.)*

- Another usage is in order to say *'about it'* or *'about them'*. For example: **Que penses-tu de mon plan? Qu'en penses-tu?** *(What do you think about my plan? What do you think about it?)*

Y

- y is used to replace words and phrases beginning with à, **chez**, or **dans** to avoid repetition.

- It can mean 'there' when replacing **dans** (in) or **sur** (on). **Il y passe tout l'été.** *(He spends the whole summer there.)*

- It can also be used to mean 'to it' or 'to them'. J'y réponds. (I'm responding to it.)

Word order for en and y

- In most cases, **en** and **y** come before the verb.
- When used in commands or instructions, en and y come AFTER the verb and is connected with a hyphen.

Examples: **restez-y** *(stay there)* / **prenez-en** *(take some)*

- en and y comes after direct or indirect object pronouns.

Example: Elle m'en a parlé. (She spoke to me about it.)

LET'S PRACTICE!

Exercise 9.1 - Answer with en or y.

1. Q: Est-ce que vous prenez du vin avec votre plat Do you take some wine with you dish? (Do you wish to take some wine with your dish?)

   A: Oui, _____

   B: Non, _____

2. Tu as de l'argent? (Do you have some money?)

   Oui, _____

   Non, _____

Replace by y or en

3. Ils sortent du cinéma à 10h. (They come out from the movie theater at 10pm.)

4. Ils vont à la maison. (They are going to their house.)

5. Ils viennent de la bibliothèque. (They are coming from the library.)

6. Les échecs? Je ne sais pas _ jouer. (Chess? I don't know how to play.)

> **Fun fact:** *Non-French celebrities who speak French include Jodie Foster, Johnny Depp, Diane Kruger, Elton John, Ewan Mcgregor, Halle Berry, Jackie O, Madonna, Mick Jagger, and John Travolta.*

Exercise 9.2 - Choose the correct answer:

1- Demain, je vais chez le dentiste. J'__ vais tous les ans. (Tomorrow, I'm going to the dentist. I go there every year)

   a. en   b.y

2- Tu peux __ aller en train. (You can go there by train.)

   a. en   b. y

3- Je m'__ sert pour travailler. (I use it to work.)

   a. en   b. y

4- Nous __ sommes fiers. (We are proud of it.)

   a. en   b. y

5- J'__ ai pensé. (I thought about it.)

   a. en   b. y

Exercise 9.3 - Complete these sentences with "en" and "y":

1- "Veux-tu du café?" "Non, je n'__ veux pas, merci." ("Do you want some coffee?" "No, thank you.")

2- Je pars à Paris ce soir. J'__ vais en train. (I'm going to Paris tonight. I'm going there by train.)

3- "As-tu assez d'argent?" "Oui, j'__ ai assez." ("Do you have enough money?" "Yes, I do.")

4- C'est un bon restaurant. Allez-__. (It's a good restaurant. Go ahead.)

5- "Vous avez encore du croissant?" "Oui, nous __ avons." ("Do you still have some croissant?" "Yes, we do.")

Exercise 9.4 - Replace the underlined words with "en" and "y":

1- Ils vont à la maison. (They go to the house.)

2- Je vais manger du gâteau. (I'm going to eat some cake.)

3- Je bois du vin très souvent. (I drink wine very often.)

4- Je crois à cette histoire. (I believe in this story.)

5- Il veut aller à Nice. (He wants to go to Nice.)

Exercise 9.5 - Answer these questions using "en" and "y":

1- Êtes-vous allés à Paris? (Did you go to Paris?)

2- Veux-tu du gâteau ? (Would you like some cake?)

3- As-tu acheté du pain ? (Did you buy bread?)

4- Avec qui vas-tu au cinéma ? (With whom do you go to the cinema?)

5- Quand vas-tu à l'école? (When are you going to school?)

ANSWERS:

Exercise 9.1

Track 28

Answer with en or y.

1/ A: Oui, j'en prends. B: Non, je n'en prends pas. 2/ Oui, j'en ai Non, je n'en ai pas

Replace by y or en

3/ Ils en sortent. 4/ Ils y vont. 5/ Ils en viennent. 6/ Les échecs? Je ne sais pas y jouer.

Exercise 9.2

1/ y 2/ y 3/ en 4/ en 5/y

Exercise 9.3

1/ en 2/ y 3/ en 4/ y 5/ en

Exercise 9.4

1/ Ils y vont. 2/ Je vais en manger. 3/ J'en bois très souvent. 4/ J'y crois. 5/ Il veut y aller.

Exercise 9.5

Example answers :

1/ Oui, nous y sommes allés. Or Non, nous n'y sommes pas allés. 2/ Oui, j'en veux. Or Non, je n'en veux pas. 3/ Oui, j'en ai acheté. Or Non, je n'en ai pas acheté. 4/ J'y vais avec mes amis. (I go there with my friends) 5/ J'y vais dans 30 minutes. (I'm going there in 30 minutes)

LESSON 10: Expressing Causes and Results

Because... It's important.

Whether you're stating your reasons, making an explanation, or discussing the cause and effect of a certain thing, you need these four words to help you out: **parce que, car, puisque**, and **comme**. They're similar, but not identical, but the important thing is they're quite easy to use.

Here are some tips for you.

- **Parce que** means 'because' in English. Like its counterpart, it is used to explain the reason why something was done or to state the motive and cause.
- It can be used in the beginning of a sentence.
- It is a subordinating conjunction and can join two parts of a sentence together.

> Example: **Je ne suis pas allé <u>parce que</u> j'étais malade.**
> *(I did not go because I was sick.)*

- **Car** also means because or for.
- It is considered very formal and not used as often as **parce que**. In fact, you're likely to find **car** in written or formal French speech only.
- You cannot begin a sentence with the word **car**, unlike **parce que**.

> Example: **Le mariage fut annulée <u>car</u> le marié est malade.**
> *(The wedding was canceled because the groom was sick.)*

- **Puisque** can be translated also as because or since.
- It can be used at the start of the sentence.
- It is used when stating very obvious reasons.

> Example: **<u>Puisque</u> tu es malade, tu peux partir.**
> *(Since you are sick, you can go.)*

- The fourth one is **comme**, which also means 'since' or 'as'.

- It is mostly found in the beginning of a sentence.

- You use it when you want to emphasize the connection between the cause and its effect.

   Example: **Comme il est malade, il peut partir.**

   (As he is sick, he can leave.)

LET'S PRACTICE!

Exercise 10.1 - Choose the right connector between « parce que » « car » « puisque » « comme » :

1- Elle a dû payé une amende ___elle a conduit trop vite. (She had to pay a fine because she drove too fast.)

2- ___ tu es en retard, tu n'iras pas au cinéma. (Since you are late, you cannot go to the movie theater.)

3- La rue Vaugirard est fermé ___ il y a une manifestation. (The Vaugirard Street is closed because there is a protest.)

4- ___ il neige, je ne peux pas aller à l'école. (As it snows, I cannot go to school.)

5- Le match fut annulée ___ la météo était mauvaise. (The game was cancelled because the weather was bad.)

Fun fact: *France has the highest number of ski resorts in the world.*

Exercise 10.2 - Choose the correct answer

1- Which one of these words cannot be placed in the beginning of a sentence?

   a. parce que   b. comme   c. puisque   d. car

2- Which one of these is more formal?

   a. car   b. parce que

3- Which one of these is used when stating very obvious reasons?

   a. parce que   b. comme   c. puisque   d. car

4- Which one of these is mostly found in the beginning of a sentence?

   a. parce que   b. comme   c. puisque   d. car

5- Which one of these is used to emphasize the connection between the cause and its effect?

   a. parce que   b. puisque   c. car   d. comme

Exercise 10.3 - Use « parce que » to link each group of two sentences:

1- Je suis en train de réviser/ j'ai un examen demain. (I'm studying/ I have an exam tomorrow)

2- Il va au restaurant/ il a faim. (He goes to a restaurant/ he's hungry)

3- Elle va au cinéma/ elle veut regarder un film. (She goes to the cinema/ she wants to see a movie)

4- Nous allons au supermarché/ nous n'avons plus de lait. (We go to the supermarket/ we don't have milk anymore)

5- Je vais chez le médecin/ je ne me sens pas très bien. (I'm going to the doctor/ I don't feel very good)

Exercise 10.4 - Use « car » to link each group of two sentences:

1- Je ne suis pas allé à l'école/ Je suis malade. (I didn't go to school/ I am sick)

2- Je ne prends pas mon petit déjeuner/ Je n'ai pas le temps. (I don't take my breakfast/ I don't have time)

3- Je visite ma grand-mère/ Elle est malade. (I visit my grandmother/ she's sick)

4- Elle boit de l'eau/ Elle a soif. (She drinks water/ she's thirsty)

5- Il achète un ordinateur/ Il en a besoin. (He buys a computer/ he needs it)

Exercise 10.5 - Use « puisque » to link each group of two sentences:

1- Je reste à la maison/ il pleut dehors. (I stay at home/ it's raining outside)

2- Je n'utilise pas mon téléphone portable/ il est cassé. (I don't use my phone/ it's broken)

3- Il ne peut pas acheter une nouvelle voiture/ il n'a pas assez d'argent. (He can't buy a new car/ he doesn't have enough money)

4- Je prends un taxi/ ma voiture est en panne. (I take a taxi/ my car broke down)

Exercise 10.6 - Use « comme » to link each group of two sentences:

1- On a allumé la cheminée/ Il fait froid dehors. (We lit a fire in the fireplace/ it's cold outside)

2- Nous allons à la plage/ Il fait chaud. (We go to the beach/ the weather is hot)

3- Il se promène dans le parc/ Il fait beau. (He takes a walk in the park/ the weather is nice)

4- Nous partons en voyage/ C'est les vacances. (We're going to travel/ it's the holidays)

Exercise 10.7 - Say if the underlined statement is a cause or a result:

1- <u>Je prends le métro</u> car c'est loin. (I take the metro to go to school because it's far away.)

2- Je lui achète un cadeau <u>parce que c'est son anniversaire</u>. (I bought him a gift because it's his birthday.)

3- <u>Comme c'est dimanche</u>, il va au musée. (Since it's Sunday, he goes to the museum.)

Exercise 10.8 - Complete these sentences with « parce que », « car », « puisque » ou « comme » :

1- ___ il était tard, nous avons décidé de rentrer. (Since it was late, we decided to go home.)

2- Je veux aller à Paris ___ je veux voir la tour Eiffel. (I want to go to Paris to see the Eifel tower.)

3- Pourquoi ne pas sortir aujourd'hui ___ il fait beau ? (Why not go out today since the weather is good?)

Exercise 10.9 - Choose an element from "column a" and another from "column b" to create a sentence:

Column a	Column b
1- J'ai fait un gâteau au chocolat	a- Car j'aime la couleur rouge.
2- J'ai acheté une robe rouge	b- Puisqu'elle est malade.
3- Elle doit se faire soigner	c- parce que j'aime le chocolat.

ANSWERS:

Exercise 10.1

Track 29

1/ Elle a dû payé une amende parce qu'elle a conduit trop vite. 2/ Puisque tu es en retard, tu n'iras pas au cinema. 3/ La rue Vaugirard est fermé car il y a une manifestation. 4/ Comme il neige, je ne peux pas aller à l'école. 5/ Le match fut annulée car la météo était mauvaise.

Exercise 10.2

1/ car 2/ car 3/ puisque 4/ comme 5/ puisque

Exercise 10.3

1/ Je suis en train de réviser car j'ai un examen demain. 2/ Il va au restaurant parce qu'il a faim. 3/ Elle va au cinéma parce qu'elle veut regarder un film. 4/ Nous allons au supermarché parce que nous n'avons plus de lait. 5/ Je vais chez le médecin parce que je ne me sens pas très bien.

Exercise 10.4

1/ Je ne suis pas allé à l'école car je suis malade. 2/ Je ne prends pas mon petit déjeuner car je n'ai pas le temps. 3/ Je visite ma grand-mère car elle est malade. 4/ Elle boit de l'eau car elle a soif. 5/ Il achète un ordinateur car il en a besoin.

Exercise 10.5

1/ Je reste à la maison puisqu'il pleut dehors. 2/ Je n'utilise pas mon téléphone portable puisqu'il est cassé. 3/ Il ne peut pas acheter une nouvelle voiture puisqu'il n'a pas assez d'argent. 5/ Je prends un taxi puisque ma voiture est en panne.

Exercise 10.6

1/ Comme il fait froid dehors, on a allumé la cheminée. 2/ Comme il fait beau, nous allons à la plage. 3/ Comme il fait beau, il se promène dans le parc. 4/ Comme c'est les vacances, nous partons en voyage.

Exercise 10.7

1/ a result 2/ a cause 3/ a cause

Exercise 10.8

1/ comme 2/ parce que/car 3/ puisque

Exercise 10.9

1/ c 2/ a 3/ b

LESSON 11: Directions and Locations

(to make sure you never get lost)

Knowing how to ask for the right direction is, of course, something highly useful to acquire. This is especially if you're planning to take a little jaunt to a French-speaking country anytime soon. If not, don't despair, it's still an important part of learning a new language.

Here is a handy guide about the words and phrases you need to know when asking for and giving directions, and for locating things.

But first, here's how to ask the right things.

Begin with:

Track 30

Où se trouve _____?

This is pronounced as 'oo-stroov' and means *Where is the* _____*?* Then insert the name of the places you're trying to locate.

Some common examples:

• l'aéroport	the airport	• le musée	the museum
• l'hôtel ___	the ___ hotel	• le restaurant	the restaurant
• la gare?	the train station	• le théâtre	the theater
• la gare routière	the bus station	• l'école	the school
• le centre-ville	the town center	• le parc	the park
• la banque	the bank	• l'épicerie	the grocery store
• les w.c.	the bathroom	• l'église	the church
• l'hôpital	the hospital	• le bureau de change	the money changer

The answers could be either of the following directions:

Track 31

• à gauche	on/to the left	• avant le/la____	before the_____
• tournez à gauche	turn left	• repérez le/la__	watch for the ___
• à droite	on/to the right	• intersection	intersection
• tournez à droite	turn right	• en haut	up
• tout droit	straight	• en bas	down
• en face	facing / across from	• près de	near to
• à côté de	next to	• loin de	far from
• devant	in front of	• au nord	to the north
• derrière	behind, at the back of	• au sud	to the south
• vers le/la_____	towards the_____	• à l'est	to the east
• après le/la ___	past the_____	• à l'ouest	to the west
• en haut	uphill	• rue	street
• en bas	downhill		

With this guide, you're unlikely to get lost in any French-speaking country anytime soon. At least, I hope not!

BONUS!!!

How about directions in a smaller scale, such as when you want to know where something is located inside a room? Here are other useful terms for you to take note of.

Track 32

Question: **où est** _____? (Where is _____?)

le téléphone portable	the cellphone
le livre	the book
la télécommande	the remote control
mon sac	my bag
la clé	the key
mon portefeuille	my wallet
l'ordinateur	the computer
l'ordinateur portable	the laptop computer

Here are the possible answers:	
sur	on top of
sous	under
devant	in front of
derrière	behind
à côté de	beside/next to
entre	between

LET'S PRACTICE!

Exercise 11.1 - Choose the right answer:

1- près de

    a. near to   b. next to

    c. straight ahead   d. far from

2- Allez tout droit.

    a. Go all the way right.   b. Go all the way.

    c. Go straight.   d. Go very far.

3- C'est à gauche.

    a. It's on the right.   b. It's straight ahead.

    c. It's on the left.   d. It's far away.

4- Où est la bibliothèque?

    a. Is there a library?   b. What time does the library?

    c. Where is the library?   d. Is the library?

5- The bank is not next to the movie theater.

    a. Le bureau de change n'est pas à côté du cinéma.

    b. La banque est à côté du cinéma.

    c. La banque n'est pas à côté du cinéma.

    d. La banque n'est pas à côté de l'école.

Fun fact: *French women have the highest life expectancy of any demographic group in the European Union.*

Exercise 11.2 - Choose the correct translation:

1- La banque est en face du parc.

    a. The bank is across from the park.   b. The bank is near the park

    c. The bank is far from park

2- Tournez à droite. Vous trouverez l'hôtel.

    a. Turn left. You'll find the hotel.   b. Turn right. You'll find the hotel.

    c. Turn right. The hotel is near.

3- Continuez tout droit.

    a. Go straight.   b. Continue all right.   c. Turn right.

Exercise 11.3 - Translate these sentences from French to English:

1- La station de train est à côté du parc.

2- L'épicerie est en face de l'école.

3- Continuez tout droit. Puis, tournez à gauche à la prochaine intersection. (Puis = then, prochaine = next)

Exercise 11.4 - Choose the correct translation:

1- The book is under the keys.

    a. Les clés sont sous le livre.   b. Le livre est sous les clés.

    c. Le livre est sur les clés.

2- Où est la télécommande portable ?

    a. Where is the remote control?   b. Where is the television?

    c. The remote control is in front of the television.

3- Mon portefeuille est sur mon sac.

    a. My wallet is in my bag.   b. My wallet is on my bag.

    c. My wallet is under my bag.

Exercise 11.5 - Complete the sentences with these words : à gauche, à droite, tout droit, en face de and loin de : (each word is used at most once)

1- Le théâtre est près de la banque. Il est juste ___ elle.

2- Tournez ___ !

3- Continuez ___.

4- L'hôpital est ___ ici.

Exercise 11.6 - Translate these sentences from English to French:

1- The cellphone is on the book.

2- The book is in front of the bag.

3- The keys are next to the computer.

Exercise 11.7 - Complete the sentences with these words : à côté, entre and devant :

1- Mon téléphone portable est ___ mon ordinateur et mon sac.

2- Tes clés sont ___ de ton sac.

3- La télécommande est ___ la télé. (télé = télévision)

ANSWERS:

Exercise 11.1

1/ near to 2/ Go straight. 3/ It's on the left. 4/ Where is the library? 5/ La banque n'est pas à côté du cinéma.

Exercise 11.2

1/ The bank is across from the park. 2/ Turn right. You'll find the hotel. 3/ Go straight.

Exercise 11.3

1/ The train station is next to the park. 2/ The grocery store is across from the school. 3/ Go straight. Then, turn left at the next intersection.

Exercise 11.4

1/ Le livre est sous les clés. 2/ Where is the remote control? 3/ My wallet is on my bag.

Exercise 11.5

1/ en face d' 2/ à gauche or à droite 3/ tout droit 4/ loin d'

Exercise 11.6

1/ Le téléphone portable est sur le livre. 2/ Le livre est devant le sac. 3/ Les clés sont près de l'ordinateur.

Exercise 11.7

1/ entre 2/ à côté 3/ devant

Day 12: Using Avoir in Perfect Tense (Passé Composé)

LESSON 12: Using Avoir in Perfect Tense (Passé Composé)

Before we jump to anything else, let's start by talking about the French perfect tense. It is also known as Passé Composé or compound past because it consists of two parts: an auxiliary verb and the past participle.

We use the perfect tense to talk about an action that was fully completed in the past. In English, it can be identified by the word 'have' that accompanies it. For example: I have eaten. The verb consists of two parts too: have and eaten. It basically works the same way in French.

The auxiliary verbs that accompany the perfect tense could either be **avoir** (to have) or être (to be). For this lesson, we will focus on **avoir**.

Here are the most important things you should know when using avoir in the perfect tense.

* avoir is used more often than être. (see the next lesson for when to use être)
* This is the format to use when forming the perfect tense with avoir:

The present tense of the verb avoir + the past participle.

* Choose from the following present tense forms of avoir:

1st person singular	j'ai	(I have)
2nd person singular	**tu as**	(you have)
3rd person singular	**il/elle a**	(he has or she has)
1st person plural	**nous avons**	(we have)
2nd person plural	**vous avez**	(you have)
3rd person plural	**ils/elles ont**	(they have)

Now, to form the past participle, here are the rules.

* First, start with the infinitive of the verb, and then proceed to the following changes in the ending.
* If the infinitive ends with an -er, replace the -er with -é.
* Examples: donner becomes donné, tomber becomes tombé

- If the infinitive ends with an -ir, remove the r at the end
- Examples: finir becomes fini, partir becomes parti
- If the infinitive ends with a -re, replace the -re with -u.
- Examples: attendre becomes attendu, descendre becomes descendu.

Using the formula above, let us take a look at a few examples:

Track 33

Pronoun + avoir	+ past participle	=perfect tense formed	meaning in English
J'ai	donné	J'ai donné	I have given.
Tu as	donné	tu as donné	You have given.

LET'S PRACTICE!

Exercise 12.1 - Give the passé composé of the verb indicated in parentheses:

1. Tu _____ du jus d'orange? (boire)

2. J' _____ de nouveaux poèmes. (écrire)

3. Nous _____ le match de foot. (regarder)

4. Jean et David _____ leurs parents hier soir. (rencontrer)

5. Il _____ beaucoup de gâteaux pour la fête. (préparer)

6. Luc _____ visite à Lisa. (rendre)

7. Cédric et Julie _____ du shopping hier. (faire)

8. Est-ce que vous _____ les moteurs? (voir)

> **Fun fact:** *Wearing a white wedding dress is a French tradition which began in 1499.*

Exercise 12.2 - Conjugate the verb « avoir » in the present tense :

Je ____

Tu ____

Il/Elle ____

Nous ____

Vous ____

Ils/Elles ____

Exercise 12.3 - Conjugate the verb « donner » (to give), « finir » (to finish) and « boire » (to drink) in perfect tense:

	Donner	Finir	Boire
Je			
Tu			
Il/elle			
Nous			
Vous			
Ils/elles			

Exercise 12.4 - Conjugate the verbs between brackets in perfect tense:

1- Nous (boire) ____ quelques verres ensemble. (We drank some glasses together)

2- Je (écrire) ____ une lettre à ma petite amie. (I wrote a letter to my girlfriend)

3- Vous (regarder) ____ le match de foot d'hier? (Did you watch yesterday's football game ?)

4- Je (rencontrer) ____ ma meilleure amie quand j'étais enfant. (I met my best friend when I was a kid)

5- Ils (préparer) ____ un gâteau d'anniversaire pour leur sœur. (They made a birthday cake for their sister)

Exercise 12.5 - Change the pronouns from plural to singular and rewrite the sentences:

1- Nous avons rendu visite à notre tante. (We visited our aunt.)

2- Bravo! Vous avez fait des progrès ! (Congratulations! You have made progress!)

3- Ils ont vu le nouveau film de Superman. (They saw the new Superman movie.)

4- Qu'est-ce que vous avez mangé hier soir ? (What did you eat yesterday?)

5- Elles ont monté les escaliers. (They went up the stairs.)

Exercise 12.6 - These sentences are given in the simple present tense. Change them into perfect tense:

1- Je perds mon temps. (I'm wasting my time.)

2- Il lit un livre. (He reads a book.)

3- Ils réalisent leurs rêves. (They realize their dreams.)

4- Est-ce que vous y croyez? (Do you believe it?)

5- Qu'est-ce que tu prépares? (What are you preparing?)

ANSWERS:

Exercise 12.1

Track 34

1/ Tu as bu du jus d'orange? 2/ J'ai écrit de nouveaux poèmes. 3/ Nous avons regardé. 4/ Jean et David ont rencontré leurs parents hier soir. 5/ Il a préparé beaucoup de gâteaux pour la fête. 6/ Luc a rendu visite à Lisa. 7/ Cédric et Julie ont fait du shopping hier. 8/ Est-ce que vous avez vu les moteurs?

Exercise 12.2:

J'ai / Tu as / Il/Elle a / Nous avons / Vous avez / Ils/Elles ont

Exercise 12.3

	Donner	Finir	Boire
Je	ai donné	ai fini	ai bu
Tu	as donné	as fini	as bu
Il/elle	a donné	a fini	a bu
Nous	avons donné	avons fini	avons bu
Vous	avez donné	avez fini	avez bu
Ils/elles	ont donné	ont fini	ont bu

Exercise 12.4

1/ Nous avons bu quelques verres ensemble. 2/ J'ai écrit une lettre à ma petite amie. 3/ Vous avez regardé le match de foot d'hier ? 4/ J'ai rencontré ma meilleure amie quand j'étais enfant. 5/ Ils ont préparé un gâteau d'anniversaire pour leur sœur.

Exercise 12.5

1/ J'ai rendu visite à ma tante. 2/ Bravo ! Tu as fait des progrès! 3/ Il a vu le nouveau film de Superman. 4/ Qu'est-ce que tu as mangé hier soir? 5/ Elle a monté les escaliers.

Exercise 12.6

1/ J'ai perdu mon temps. 2/ Il a lu un livre. 3/ Ils ont réalisés leurs rêves. 4/ Est-ce que vous y avez cru? 5/ Qu'est-ce que tu as préparé ?

Day 13: Using être in Perfect Tense (Passé Composé)

LESSON 13: Using être in Perfect Tense (Passé Composé)

While the previous lesson explored using avoir in forming the perfect tense, for this one we will focus on the second auxiliary verb in the perfect tense: être.

Here are the important things to remember:

• The format is quite similar to the previous one.

The present tense of the verb être + the past participle.

• These are the present tense forms of être together with the corresponding pronouns.
    • Je suis
    • tu es
    • il est
    • nous somes
    • vous êtes
    • ils sont

As mentioned in lesson 12, être is not used as often as avoir in the perfect tense. Given this, the question is, when do you use it?

There are two groups of verbs that makes use of être, and these are:

1. Reflexive verbs

When we say reflexive verbs, we mean the French verbs that appear with the pronoun se or the shortened form s' before it. These action words are used when the subject is the same person as the object. To put it simply, it means "to____ oneself".

Take, for example, the verb habiller which means to get dressed.

Track 35

Pronoun + être	+ past participle	perfect tense formed	meaning in English
je me suis	**habillé**	**je me suis habillé**	(I got dressed)
tu t'es	**habillé**	**tu t'es habillé**	(you got dressed)
il s'est	**habillé**	**il s'est habillé**	(he got dressed)
elle s'est	**habillée**	**elle s'est habillée**	(she got dressed)
nous nous sommes	**habillés**	**nous nous sommes habillés**	(we got dressed)
vous vous êtes	**habillés**	**vous vous êtes habillés**	(you got dressed)
ils se sont	**habillés**	**ils se sont habillés**	(they got dressed)

2. A selected group of verbs that mostly refer to or involve bodily movement or some kind of physical activity.

Track 36

Some common examples:

aller (to go)	**descendre** (to go down)	**mourir** (to die)	**tomber** (to fall)
venir (to come)	**monter** (to go up)	**naître** (to be born)	**retourner** (to go back/ return)
arriver (to arrive)	**entrer** (to go in/ come in)	**devenir** (to become)	**rentrer** (to come back/ come home)
partir (to leave/go)	**sortir** (to go out)	**rester** (to stay)	

Even more rules:

- To form the past participle when using être, the past participle has to agree with the subject of the verb.

Therefore, their endings change to accommodate the masculine and feminine, as well as the singular and plural forms.

Here are the two steps to form the past participle for verbs that use être.

Step 1: Change the infinitive

- If the infinitive ends with an -er, replace the -er with -é.
- If the infinitive ends with an -ir, remove the r at the end.
- If the infinitive ends with a -re, replace the -re with -u.

Step 2: Add the correct endings

- To form a masculine plural past participle, you add -s
- To form a feminine singular past participle, you add -e
- To form a feminine plural past participle, you add -es

Examples:

	Masculine endings	Examples	Feminine Endings	Examples
Singular	-	tombé parti descendu	-e	tombée
Plural	-s	tombés partis descendus	-es	tombées parties descendues

Some examples using the format.

Track 37

Je suis tombé. (masculine)	I have fallen.	Je suis tombée. (feminine)
Tu es tombé. (masculine)	You have fallen.	Tu es tombée. (feminine)
Il est tombé.	He/it has fallen. She/it has fallen (for elle...)	Elle est tombée.
Nous sommes tombés. (masculine)	We have fallen.	Nous sommes tombées. (feminine)
Vous êtes tombés. (masculine)	You have fallen.	Vous êtes tombées. (feminine)
Ils sont tombés.	They have fallen.	Elles sont tombées. (feminine)

LET'S PRACTICE!

Exercise 13.1 - Give the passé composé of the verb indicated in parentheses:

1. Cyril en France il y a un an. (aller)

2. Pierre _____ en retard, comme toujours. (arriver)

3. Hier Julie _____ dans le cours de Yoga. (tomber)

4. Je _____ à la maison hier soir. (rester)

5. Vous _____ très tard après la fête. (rentrer)

6. Dominique et Sophie_____ ensemble. (venir)

7. Marie_____ en mai. (naître)

8. Pourquoi est-ce que vous _____ avec Bette? (partir)

> **Fun fact:** *There are more than 1000 different kinds of cheese made in France.*

Exercise 13.2 - Conjugate the verb « être » in the present tense :

Je ____

Tu ____

Il/Elle ____

Nous ____

Vous ____

Ils/Elles ____

Exercise 13.3: Conjugate the verb « s'habiller » (to get dressed up), « se laver » (to wash oneself) and « se coucher » (to go to bed) in perfect tense. What are these verbs called?

	S'habiller	Se laver	Se coucher
Je			
Tu			
Il			
Elle			
Nous			
Vous			
Ils			
Elles			

Exercise 13.4 - Conjugate the verbs between brackets in perfect tense:

1- Il (venir) ___ tout seul. (He came alone.)

2- Nous (sortir) ___ ensemble l'année dernière. (We went out together last year.)

3- Je (reste) ___ à la maison hier. (I stayed home yesterday.)

4- Elle (naître) ___ le 10 décembre. (She was born on December 10th.)

5- Vous (aller) ___ à l'école ? (Did you go to school?)

Exercise 13.5 - Change the pronouns from plural to singular and rewrite the sentences:

1- Ils sont devenus vieux. (They became old.)

2- Elles sont parties hier. (They left yesterday.)

3- Vous êtes arrivés quand? (When did you arrive?)

4- Nos voitures sont tombées en panne. (Our cars broke down.)

5- Nous sommes tombés de la falaise. (We fell off the cliff.)

Exercise 13.6 - These sentences are given in the simple present tense. Change them into perfect tense:

1- Je vais à la maison. (I go to the house.)

2- Il entre dans la salle. (He enters the room.)

3- Je sors acheter du pain. (I go out to buy bread.)

4- Elles rentrent tard. (I come home late.)

5- Tu pars quand? (When do you leave?)

ANSWERS:

Exercise 13.1

Track 38

1/ Cyril est allé en France il y a un an. 2/ Pierre est arrivé en retard, comme toujours. 3/ Hier Julie est tombée dans le cours de Yoga. 4/ Je suis resté à la maison hier soir. 5/ Vous êtes rentrés très tard après la fête. 6/ Dominique et Sophie sont venues ensemble. 7/ Marie est née en mai. 8/ Pourquoi est-ce que vous êtes partis avec Bette?

Exercise 13.2

Je suis

Tu es

Il/Elle est

Nous sommes

Vous êtes

Ils/Elles sont

Exercise 13.3

	S'habiller	Se laver	Se coucher
Je	me suis habillé	me suis lavé	me suis couché
Tu	t'es habillé	t'es lavé	t'es couché
Il	s'est habillé	s'est lavé	s'est couché
Elle	s'est habillée	s'est lavée	s'est couchée
Nous	nous sommes habillés	nous sommes lavés	nous sommes couchés
Vous	vous êtes habillés	vous êtes lavés	
Ils	se sont habillés	se sont lavés	vous êtes couchés
Elles	se sont habillées	se sont lavées	se sont couchés
			se sont couchées

These are called reflexive verbs.

Exercise 13.4

1/ Il est venu tout seul. 2/ Nous sommes sortis ensemble l'année dernière. 3/Je suis resté(e) à la maison hier. 4/ Elle est née le 10 décembre. 5/ Vous êtes allés à l'école ?

Exercise 13.5

1/ Il est devenu vieux. 2/ Elle est partie hier. 3/ Tu es arrivé quand? 4/ Ma voiture est tombée en panne. 5/ Je suis tombé(e) de la falaise.

Exercise 13.6

1/ Je suis allé(e) à la maison. 2/ Il est entré dans la salle. 3/ Je suis sorti acheter du pain. 4/ Elles sont rentrées tard. 5/ Tu es parti quand ?

Day 14: The Imperfect Tense

LESSON 14: The Imperfect Tense

...or when past events aren't directly specified

We call it *imparfait*. It is the verb tense used to talk about past events, especially in descriptions. Unlike the perfect tense, which is used for events that were fully completed, the imperfect tense does not imply a beginning or ending of an action.

In English, you're probably unaware it even exists. Unlike other romantic languages, English doesn't make use of the imperfect tense, but rather uses the past progressive to denote continuous action and the simple past to express a previous state.

We use the imperfect tense:

- To give a physical or emotional description of a past event. (Example: It was raining so hard)
- To talk about a past habitual occurrence or state of being. (Example: I used to like her a lot.)
- To indicate an action that was ongoing when something else took place. (Example: We were walking our dog when the aliens came.)

In English, we simply say was ____, was ____- ing or used to____.

Here are some important stuff to keep in mind when forming the imperfect tense:

- To conjugate a verb into the imperfect, you only need to change the ending of the verb.
- For verbs that end in -er and -re, use the infinitive, but chop off the -er or the -re ending.

Afterwards, add the new ending based on the subject.

- For -er and -re verbs, the imperfect tense endings are -ais, -ais, -ait, -ions, -iez, -aient.
- Using the verb **donner** (to give) as an example for -er verbs, here's what happens when we add the ending:

Track 39

Je donnais	(I gave, I was giving, I used to give)
Tu donnais	(you gave, you were giving, you used to give)
Il/elle/on donnait	(he/she/one gave/ was giving/ used to give)
Nous donnions	(we gave, we were giving, we used to give)
Vous donniez	(you gave, you were giving, you used to give)
Ils/elles donnaient	(they gave, they were giving, they used to give)

- For -re verbs, let's use **attendre** (to wait). With the correct endings, here's what becomes of it in the imperfect tense:

Track 40

J'attendais	(I waited, I was waiting, I used to wait)
Tu attendais	(you waited, you were waiting, you used to wait)
Il attendait	(he/she/one waited/ was waiting/ used to wait)
Nous attendions	(we waited/ we were waiting/ we used to wait)
Vous attendiez	you waited/ you were waiting/ you used to wait)
Ils/elles attendaient	(they waited, they were waiting, they used to wait)

- For verbs than end in -ir such as **finir** (to finish), simply emove the -ir and add the appropriate endings.
- For -ir verbs, the endings are -issais, -issais, -issait, -issions, -issiez, -issaient.
- When using finir as an example, here are the results with the new endings:

Track 41

Je finissais	(I finished, I was finishing, I used to finish)
Tu finissais	(you finished, you were finishing, you used to finish),
Il/elle/on finissait	(he/she/one finished/was finishing/used to finish),
Nous finissions	(we finished, we were finishing, we used to finish)
Vous finissiez	(you finished, you were finishing, you used to finish)
Ils/elles finissaient	(they finished, they were finishing, they used to finish)

LET'S PRACTICE!

Exercise 14.1 - Give the imparfait of the verb indicated in the parenthess:

1. Jean et Luc _____ la table quand Lisa a téléphoné. (mettre)

2. Sophie _____ la biologie avant la soirée. (étudier)

3. Je _____ des noisettes quand il a commencé à pleuvoir. (ramasser)

4. J'_____ la musique classique quand David est arrivé. (écouter)

5. Nous _____ nos exercices quand le cours a commencé. (finir)

6. Tu _____ de l'alcool toute la soirée? (boire)

7. Vous _____ des rumeurs pendant le cours? (entendre)

8. Julie _____ à l'amitié de Jean quand Sophie est arrivée. (réfléchir)

> **Fun fact:** *The French national anthem is called la Marseillaise because it was first sung by soldiers from the Marseille marching to Paris.*

Exercise 14.2 - Conjugate "écouter" (to listen), "réfléchir" (to think) and "mettre» (tu put) in the imperfect tense:

	écouter	réfléchir	mettre
Je			
Tu			
Il/elle			
Nous			
Vous			
Ils/elles			

Exercise 14.3 - Conjugate the verbs between brackets in imperfect tense:

1- Je (faire) ____ le ménage pendant que mon père cuisinait. (I was doing the household chores while my dad was cooking.)

2- Il (attendre) ____ ce résultat avec impatience. (He was impatiently waiting for the results.)

3- Tous les jours, ils (courir) ____ dans le parc. (Every day, they ran in the park.)

4- Nous (chanter) ____ ensemble. (We used to sing together.)

5- Vous (être) ____ amis, n'est-ce pas? (You used to be friends, right ?)

Exercise 14.4 - Change the pronouns from singular to plural then rewrite the sentences:

1- Il était gentil. (He was kind.)

2- Je mangeais souvent dans ce restaurant quand je vivais ici. (I often ate at this restaurant when I used to live here.)

3- Elle apprenait la dance dans cet établissement. (She was learning dance in this school.)

4- Tu était inconscient. (You were unconscious.)

5- Je travaillais très dur pendant qu'il était assis à ne rien faire. (I was working very hard while he was sitting doing nothing.)

Exercise 14.5 - Change the pronouns from plural to singular then rewrite the sentences:

1- Nous grimpions à cet arbre quand nous étions enfants. (We used to climb this tree when we were kids.)

2- Vous le voyiez souvent, n'est-ce pas? (You were always seeing him, isn't it?)

3- Elles aimaient voyager en train. (They liked/used to like to travel by train.)

4- Nous allions quelquefois au cinéma. (We went/used to went to the cinema sometimes)

5- Des arbres entouraient la maison. (Trees surrounded/used to surround the house.)

Exercise 14.6 - Conjugate the verbs between brackets in imperfect tense:

1- Je (pratiquer) ___ du sport tous les jours quand j'avais le temps. (I used to practice sports every day when I had time.)

2- Le ciel (être) ___ nuageux. (The sky was cloudy.)

3- Nous (passer) ___ notre temps à lire. (We spent our time reading.)

4- Elle (prendre) ___ le bus tous les jours. (She used to take the bus every day.)

5- Mon grand-père (lire) ___ le journal tous les matins. (My grandfather used to read the newspaper every morning.)

ANSWERS:

Exercise 14.1

Track 42

1/ Jean et Luc mettaient la table quand Lisa a téléphoné. 2/ Sophie étudiait la biologie avant la soirée. 3/ Je ramassais des noisettes quand il a commencé à pleuvoir. 4/ J'écoutais la musique classique quand David est arrive. 5/ Nous finissions nos exercices quand le cours a commencé. 6/ Tu buvais de l'alcool toute la soirée? 7/ Vous entendiez des rumeurs pendant le cours? 8/ Julie réfléchissait à l'amitié de Jean quand Sophie est arrivée.

Exercise 14.2

	écouter	réfléchir	mettre
Je	écoutais	réfléchissais	mettrais
Tu	écoutais	réfléchissais	mettrais
Il/elle	écoutait	réfléchissait	mettrait
Nous	écoutions	réfléchissions	mettrions
Vous	écoutiez	réfléchissiez	mettriez
Ils/elles	écoutaient	réfléchissaient	mettraient

Exercise 14.3

1/ Je faisais le ménage pendant que mon père cuisinait. 2/ Il attendait ce résultat avec impatience. 3/ Tous les jours, ils couraient dans le parc. 4/ Nous chantions ensemble. 5/ Vous étiez amis, n'est-ce pas ?

Exercise 14.4

1/ Ils étaient gentils. 2/ Nous mangions souvent dans ce restaurant quand nous vivions ici. 3/ Elles apprenaient la dance dans cet établissement. 4/ Vous étiez inconscients. 5/ Nous travaillons très dut pendant qu'ils étaient assis à ne rien faire.

Exercise 14.5

1/ Je grimpais à cet arbre quand j'étais enfant. 2/ Tu le voyais souvent, n'est-ce pas? 3/ Elle aimait voyager en train. 4/ J'allais quelquefois au cinéma. 5/ Un arbre entourait la maison.

Exercise 14.6

1/ Je pratiquais du sport tous les jours quand j'avais le temps. 2/ Le ciel était nuageux. 3/ Nous passions notre temps à lire. 4/ Elle prenait le bus tous les jours. 5/ Mon grand-père lisait le journal tous les matins.

Day 15: THE IMPERATIVE

LESSON 15: The Imperative

Imagine a world where there are no commands or orders being given. Well, yeah, that's right, you can't. Whether you're the one telling people what to do, or you're the one on the receiving end, the world seems to run on commands.

To issue commands or give instructions, we use the imperative form of the verb.

Its other uses are:

- to express a desire (which is basically still a form of issuing a command, only said a lot more nicely)
- to make a request (a very, very polite kind of command)
- to give advice (still a form of command if we come to think of it)
- to recommend something (yup, still a command cloaked in a helpful kinda coat)

Here are a list of important things to learn about the imperative in French or the *imperatif*.

- There are three forms used for the imperative. Two are commonly-used and these correspond to **tu** and **vous**. The third form **nous** is used sometimes, and it works the same way we say "let's" in English.
- Unlike the other verb forms and grammatical moods, the imperative does not use subject pronouns. Instead, object pronouns are being used.
- To form the present tense imperative, simply use the present indicative forms for tu, nous, and vous without mentioning these pronouns.
- The conjugation is basically the same as the present tense except that for -er verbs, the last -s is dropped in the tu form.

Example for verbs ending in **-er: donner** becomes (tu) donne, (nous) donnons, (vous) donnez.

> **Donne-moi ça!** (Give me that!)

Example for verbs ending in -ir: finir becomes (tu) finis, (nous) finissons, (vous) finissez.

> **Finissez vos devoirs.** (Finish your homework.)

Example for verbs ending in **-re: attendre** becomes (tu) attends, (nous) attendons, (vous) attendez.

> **Attendons le bus.** (Let's wait for the bus.)

- There are two kinds of commands where the imperative is being used: **the affirmative commands** and the **negative commands.** The affirmative command would be like "Do this!" while the negative command is its opposite "Don't do that!"
- In French, the object pronoun which accompanies the imperative changes its position depending on the kind of command being issued.

Track 43

- For affirmative commands, the object pronouns come after the verb. The verb and the pro-noun are then linked together with a hyphen.

> Example: **Excusez-moi.** (Excuse me.)

- For negative commands, the object pronouns come before the verb. And **ne... pas** is used.

> Example: **Ne leur parlons pas.** (Don't speak to them.)

- In cases where both direct and indirect object pronouns are present, the DIRECT OBJECT PRONOUNS always come BEFORE the INDIRECT OBJECT PRONOUNS.

> Example: **Donnez-la-nous!** (Give it to us!)

Direct object pronouns	le, la, les
Indirect object pronouns	**moi, toi, lui, nous, vous, leur**

LET'S PRACTICE!

Exercise 15.1 - Fill in the blanks with the imperative form of the verb between parentheses:

1- _____ Jean! On étaient si heureux à Lyon! (se rappeler)

2- Lisa, _____ tes légumes! (finir)

3- _____ de nous disputer! (arrêter)

4- _____ prétentieux, David! (ne pas être)

5- _____ rester modestes! (savoir)

6- _____ chez le coiffeur Benjamin! (aller)

7- Tu as envie d'aller chez ta copine, Jean? _____-y! (aller)

8- J'achète de la bière? David : Oui,_____-en plusieurs bouteilles! (acheter)

> **Fun fact:** *The Statue of Liberty was made in France and then gifted to the U.S on the celebration of the country's centennial year in 1886.*

Exercise 15.2 - Conjugate "écouter" (to listen), "réfléchir" (to think) and "mettre» (tu put) in the imperative tense:

	écouter	réfléchir	mettre
(Tu)			
(Nous)			
(Vous)			

Exercise 15.3 - Conjugate the verbs between brackets in imperative tense:

1- ___-toi les mains avant de manger (laver). (Wash your hands before you eat.)

2- ___ bien ce que je vous dis. (écouter) (Listen well to what I'm telling you.)

3- ___ vos ceintures. (attacher) (Fasten your seatbelts.)

4- ___ confiance en moi ! (avoir) (Trust me.)

5- ___ à gauche à la prochaine intersection, puis continuez tout droit. (tourner) (Turn left at the next intersection, then continue straight.)

Exercise 15.4 - Change the pronouns from singular to plural and rewrite the sentences:

1- Dépêche-toi. On va être en retard. (Hurry up. We're going to be late.)

2- Finis ta soupe. (Finish your soup.)

3- Prends le bus. C'est plus rapide. (Take the bus. It's faster.)

4- Sois à l'heure la prochaine fois. (Be on time next time.)

5- Viens avec moi. (Come with me.)

Exercise 15.5 - These sentences are given in the simple present tense form. Change them into imperative tense and do the necessary changes:

1- Il mange ses légumes. (He eats his vegetables.)

2- Elle me donne son numéro. (She gives me her number.)

3- Ils éteignent la lumière avant de sortir de la salle. (They turn off the light before they leave the room.)

4- Nous partons en vacances cet été. (We're going on vacation this summer.)

5- Il téléphone au directeur. (He calls the director.)

Exercise 15.6 - Change the pronouns from plural to singular and rewrite the sentences:

1- Prenez soin de vous-même. (Take care of yourselves.)

2- Souhaitez-moi bonne chance. (Wish me good luck.)

3- Envoyez-moi un email. (Send me an email.)

4- Entendez-vous un bruit? (Do you hear a sound?)

5- Ne vous découragez pas! (Don't be discouraged!)

Exercise 15.7 - Conjugate the verbs between brackets in imperative tense:

1- ___-moi un café, s'il vous plait. (donner) (Give me a coffee, please.)

2- ___ ta chambre tout de suite ! (ranger) (Clean up your room immediately!)

3- ___ -moi le sel. (passer) (Hand me the salt.)

4- ___ tes devoirs avant de regarder la télé. (faire) (Do your homework before watching TV.)

5- N'___ pas d'apporter vos ordinateurs portables. (oublier) (Don't forget to bring your laptops.)

ANSWERS:

Exercise 15.1

Track 44

1/ Rappelle-toi Jean! On étaient si heureux à Lyon! (se rappeler) 2/ Lisa, finis tes légumes! (finir) 3/ Arrêtons de nous disputer! (arrêter) 4/ Ne sois pas prétentieux, David! (ne pas être) 5/ Sachons rester modestes! (savoir) 6/ Va chez le coiffeur Benjamin! (aller) 7: Tu as envie d'aller chez ta copine, Jean? Vas-y! (aller) 8/ J'achète de la bière? David : Oui, achètes-en plusieurs bouteilles! (acheter)

Exercise 15.2

	écouter	réfléchir	mettre
(Tu)	écoute	réfléchis	mets
(Nous)	écoutons	réfléchissons	mettons
(Vous)	écoutez	réfléchissez	mettez

Exercise 15.3

1/ Lave-toi les mains avant de manger. 2/ Écoutez bien ce que je vous dis. 3/ Attachez vos ceintures. 4/ Aie confiance en moi! 5/ tournez à gauche à la prochaine intersection, puis continuez tout droit.

Exercise 15.4

1/ Dépêchez-vous. On va être en retard. 2/ Finissez vos soupes. 3/ Prenez le bus. C'est plus rapide. 4/ Soyez à l'heure la prochaine fois. 5/ Venez avec moi.

Exercise 15.5

1/ Mange tes légumes. 2/ Donne-moi ton numéro. 3/ Éteignez la lumière avant de sortir de la salle. 4/ Partons en vacances cet été. 5/ Téléphone au directeur.

Exercise 15.6

1/ Prends soin de toi-même. 2/ Souhaite-moi bonne chance. 3/ Envoie-moi un email. 4/ Entends-tu un bruit? 5/ Ne te décourage pas!

Exercise 15.7

1/ Donnez-moi un café, s'il vous plait. 2/ Range ta chambre tout de suite. 3/ Passe-moi le sel. 4/ Fais tes devoirs avant de regarder la télé. 5/ N'oubliez pas d'apporter vos ordinateurs portables.

Day 16: Comparative and Superlative

LESSON 16: Comparative and Superlative

This book is awesome.

This book is more awesome than other books.

This book is the most awesome of all.

See? This book is so awesome that in three sentences it just illustrated the difference between comparative and superlative adjectives.

In both English and French, comparatives are used to compare superiority, inferiority, or equality between two or more things. As for the superlatives, we use it to talk about the extremes, like the worst or the best.

These being the descriptive words that they are, can occur both in adjectives and adverbs. We've listed the most important things you need to remember about comparatives and superlatives in French below.

First, for the ADJECTIVES:

Here are some tips and rules in using comparative adjectives:

1. Use the French word **plus** which means 'more'. For example: Cette question est **plus** facile. (This question is easier.)
2. Use the word **moins** which means 'less'. Cette veste est **moins** chère. (This jacket is less expensive.)
3. Use the word **que** which means 'than' when introducing the other person or thing you are comparing your subject with. Elle est plus petite que moi. (She's smaller than me.)
4. Use the word **aussi** paired with **que** to say your subject is similar to the other thing. In English, we use this to say, (subject) is as (adjective) as (subject 2). For example: Il est aussi inquiet que moi. (He's as worried as me.)

For superlative adjectives, here's a rundown of the things you should know:

1. You can use **plus** to mean 'most' depending on the form of the adjective you're using.

Masculine singular adjectives --- **le plus**
Feminine singular adjectives --- **la plus**
Plural adjectives (masculine and feminine) --- **les plus**

Examples:

le guide **le plus** utile (the most useful guidebook)
le question **laplus** facile (the easiest question)
les plus grands hôtels (the biggest hotels)

2. You can use **moins** to mean 'least' depending on the form of the adjective you're using.

Masculine singular adjectives --- **le moins**
Feminine singular adjectives --- **la moins**
Plural adjectives (masculine and feminine) --- **les moins**

Examples:

le guide **le moins** utile (the least useful guidebook)
le question **la moins** facile (the least easy or the hardest question)
le mois **les moins** agréables (the least pleasant months)

Now for the adverbs.

Comparatives and superlatives in adverbs work roughly the same way they do with adjectives. The main difference is that, unlike the adjectives, the superlatives of the adverbs no longer need to agree to the gender or number to the word they are describing (which makes life a lot easier, we must say).

Remember these tiny bits of information when using comparative adverbs:

1. Use **plus... que** which means *more... than.* (example: Tu marches plus vite que moi. You walk faster than me.)

2. Use **moins... que** to say *less... than.* (example: Nous nous voyons moins souvent qu'avant. We now see each other less often than before.)

3. **Use aussi... que** to say *as...as.* (example: Je parle français aussi bien que toi! I can speak French as well as you!)

For superlative adverbs, here are the things you should take note of:

1. Superlatives in adverbs work the same way as they do in the adjectives, except for one thing: you no longer need to make **le** agree with the gender or number. In short, there is no **la** or les for the feminine and plural forms. Le stays as is.

2. Use **le plus** to say the most or the ____est. (Example: Michelle parle le plus vite. Michelle speaks the fastest.)

3. Use **le moins** to say the least or the ____est. (Example: C'est Cathy qui a mangé le moins. Cathy ate the least.)

LET'S PRACTICE!

Exercise 16.1

1/ Comparatives:

Fill in the blank with the appropriate comparative of the adjective in parentheses. '+' is for 'more...than', '-' for 'less...than', and '=' for 'as... as'. Do not forget to make the adjectives agree in number and gender with the nouns they qualify.

1- L'anglais de Jean est _____ que celui de David (+, mauvais)

2- Julie a un _____ Q.I. ('I.Q.') que Sophie (+, bon)

3- Sophie est _____ que Julie. (=, joli)

4- Luc est _____ que David. (+, gentil)

5- Les Spurs sont _____ que les Heat. (-, fort)

2/ Superlative

Fill in the blank with the appropriate superlative of the adjective in parentheses. '+' is for 'the most', '-' for 'the least'. Do not forget to make the adjectives agree in number and gender with the nouns they qualify.

1- Jean a _____ accent de la classe. (+, mauvais)

2- Le Q.I. ('I.Q.') de David est _____ de l'école. (+, bon)

3- Lunq est la chatte _____ du campus. (+ mignonne)

4- Sophie est l'employée _____ du magasin (+, travailleur)

5- Les singes sont les animaux _____ du zoo. (+, mignon)

6- Les vaches sont les animaux _____ de la ferme (-, intelligent)

> **Fun fact:** *French cuisine is considered one of the best in the world and there are an average of two cookery books being published every day in the world.*

Exercise 16.2 - For each sentence, say which one is used: the comparative or the superlative:

1- Je suis plus organisée que mon frère. (I am more organized than my brother.)

2- Tu es la personne la plus gentille que je connaisse. (You're the kindest person I know.)

3- Cet arbre est le plus vieux au monde. (This tree is the oldest one in the world.)

4- Il est aussi méchant que sa femme. (He is as mean as his wife.)

5- C'est le plus beau spectacle que j'ai jamais vu. (It's the most beautiful show I've ever seen.)

Exercise 16.3 - Complete these sentences with: « plus », « moins » or « aussi » (Note (+) is for superiority, (-) is for inferiority, (=) is for equality):

1- Il est (=) ____ têtu que son frère. (He's as stubborn as his brother.)

2- Elle est (+) ____ grande que son petit copain. (She's taller than her boyfriend.)

3- Cette tâche est (-) ____ difficile que celle d'hier. (This task is less difficult than the one from yesterday.)

4- Ma chambre est (+) ____ grande que celle de ma sœur. (My room is bigger than my sister's.)

5- Il est (=) ____ séduisant que son père. (He's as attractive as his father.)

Exercise 16.4 - Complete these sentences with : « le plus », « la plus » or « les plus » :

1- Marc est la personne ____ intelligente de la famille. (Marc is the most intelligent person in the family).

2- Je trouve que les chiots sont les animaux ____ mignons au monde. (I think puppies are the cutest animals in the world.)

3- Le petit-déjeuner est le repas ____ important de la journée. (Breakfast is the most important meal of the day.)

4- Joséphine est l'élève ____ brillante de la classe. (Josephine is the brightest student in the class.)

5- Léo est l'employé ____ sérieux du magasin. (Leo is the most serious employee of the shop.)

Exercise 16.5 - Complete these sentences with : « plus », « moins », « aussi » or « que »:

1- Mon père est (+) ___ âgé ___ ma mère. (My dad is older than my mother.)

2- C'est le (+) ___ beau pays que j'ai visité. (It's the most beautiful country I visited.)

3- Il est (=) ___ maladroit ___ son fils. (He's as clumsy as his son.)

4- Ce livre est le (+) ___ intéressant que j'ai lu. (This book is the most interesting one I've read.)

5- Elle est la personne la (-) ___ paresseuse de la famille. (She's the least lazy person of the family.)

Exercise 16.6 - Use the words to create sentences:

Example : Marc/ (+) grand/ Léa ==> Marc est plus grand que léa. (Marc is taller than Lea.)

1- Les chiens/ (+) mignons/ les chats. (dogs/ (+) cute/ cats)

2- La robe bleue/ (+) jolie/ la noire. (The blue dress/ (+) pretty/ the black one)

3- Le violon/ (-) facile à apprendre/ la guitare. (Violin/ (-) easy to learn/ the guitar)

4- Marc/ (+) travailleur/ son meilleur ami. (Marc/ (+) hardworking/ his bestfriend)

5- Julie/ (=) serviable/ sa sœur. (Julie/ (=) helpful/ her sister)

Exercise 16.7 - Reorganize the words to make sentences:

Example : est l'élève la plus brillante/Marie/de sa classe ==> Marie est l'élève la plus brillante de sa classe. (Marie is the brightest student in her class.)

1- Ma mère/ que je connaisse/ est la personne la plus courageuse (My mother/ that I know/ is the most courageous person.)

2- est l'élève le plus grand/de la classe/ Paul (is the tallest student/ of the class/ Paul)

3- que j'ai jamais gouté/ C'est le gâteau/ le plus savoureux (that I've ever tasted/ it's the cake/ the most delicious tasty)

4- est le plus grand/ Ce bâtiment/ de la ville (is the tallest/ This building/ in the city)

5- C'était l'étoile/ que j'aie jamais vue/ la plus brillante (It was the star/ that I have ever seen/ the brightest)

ANSWERS:

Exercise 16.1

Track 45

Comparatives

1/ L'anglais de Jean est plus mauvais que celui de David. 2/ Julie a un meilleur Q.I. ('I.Q.') que Sophie. 3/ Sophie est aussi jolie que Julie. 4/ Luc est plus gentil que David. 5/ Les Spurs sont moins forts que les Heat.

Superlatives

1/ Jean a le plus mauvais accent de la classe. 2/ Le Q.I. ('I.Q.') de David est le meilleur de l'école. 3/ Luna est la chatte la plus mignonne du campus. 4/ Sophie est l'employée la plus travailleuse du magasin. 5/ Les singes sont les animaux les plus mignons du zoo. 6/ Les vaches sont les animaux les moins intelligents de la ferme.

Exercise 16.2

1/ Comparative 2/ Superlative 3/ Superlative 4/ Comparative 5/ Superlative

Exercise 16.3

1/ Il est aussi têtu que son frère. 2/ Elle est plus grande que son petit copain. 3/ Cette tâche est moins difficile que celle d'hier. 4/ Ma chambre est plus grande que celle de ma sœur. 5/ Il est aussi séduisant que son frère.

Exercise 16.4

1/ Marc est la personne la plus intelligente de la famille. 2/ Je trouve que les chiots sont les animaux les plus mignons au monde. 3/ Le petit-déjeuner est le repas le plus important de la journée. 4/ Joséphine est l'élève la plus brillante de la classe. 5/ Léo est l'employé le plus sérieux du magasin.

Exercise 16.5

1/ Mon père est plus âgé que ma mère. 2/ C'est le plus beau pays que j'ai visité. 3/ Il est aussi maladroit que son fils. 4/ Ce livre est le plus intéressant que j'ai lu. 5/ Elle est la personne la moins paresseuse de la famille.

Exercise 16.6

1/ Les chiens sont plus mignons que les chats. 2/ La robe bleue est plus jolie que la noire. 3/ Le violon est moins facile à apprendre que la guitare. 4/ Marc est plus travailleur que son meilleur ami. 5/ Julie est aussi serviable que sa sœur.

Exercise 16.7

1/ Ma mère est la personne la plus courageuse que je connaisse. 2/ Paul est l'élève le plus grand de la classe. 3/ C'est le gâteau le plus savoureux que j'ai jamais gouté. 4/ Ce bâtiment est le plus grand de la ville. 5/ C'était l'étoile la plus brillante que j'aie jamais vue.

Day 17: Possessive and Demonstrative Adjectives

LESSON 17: Possessive and Demonstrative Adjectives

We all know what adjectives can do (right?) These are the words that describe a noun. But their purpose is not limited to descriptions such as 'cool' or 'kind' or 'pretty'. They have a host of other uses, such as providing more information about the noun they're appearing with, or even pointing out something.

In this lesson, we'll be talking about (or rather, breezing through) possessive adjectives and demonstrative adjectives. These are relatively easy topics that won't be needing a lot of brain cell activity. So, sit back and try to enjoy today's topic.

First, **possessive adjectives**.

When you need to express that a noun belongs to another person or thing, you use possessive adjectives. We know it in English as the words: my, your, his, her, its, our, and their.

In French, the possessive adjectives (like all other kinds of adjectives) need to agree to the noun they're describing.

Here's a nifty little table to cover all that.

Track 46

When used with masculine singular noun	When used with feminine singular noun	When used with plural noun whether feminine or masculine	What it means
Mon	ma (*mon)	mes	my
Ton	ta (*ton)	tes	your
Son	sa (*son)	ses	his/her/its/one's
Notre	notre	nos	our
Votre	votre	vos	your
Leur	leur	leurs	their

Note that **mon, ton** and **son** are used in the feminine form with nouns that begin with a vowel or the letter h.

Here are some more reminders in using possessive adjectives:

• Possessive adjectives always come BEFORE the noun.
• Possessive adjectives don't 'agree' with the owner of the item being used in the sentence, but with the item itself.

In French, possessive adjectives are not used to point out body parts. **Le, la l'** or **les** are being used instead (don't ask us why)

Exercise 17.1 - Choose the correct answer:

1- __ soeur est gentille. (My sister is kind.)

    a. Ma   b. Mon   c. Mes

2- J'aime __ chien. (I love my dog.)

    a. ta   b. sa   c. ma

3- J'ai ouvert __ armoire. (I opened my wardrobe.)

    a. mon   b. ma   c. ton

4- Prends __ voiture. (Take your car.)

    a. ma   b. ta   c. ton

5- J'ai oublié __ clés. (I forgot my keys.)

    a. mon   b. ma   c. mes

Exercise 17.2 - Fill in the blanks with: mon, ma, mes:

1- __ voiture est tombée en panne. (My car broke down.)

2- Il a mangé __ yaourt. (He ate my yogurt.)

3- J'ai perdu __ lunettes. (I lost my glasses.)

4- Ils m'ont acheté un délicieux gâteau pour __ anniversaire. (They bought me a delicious cake for my birthday.)

5- __ jambes me font mal après l'entraînement. (My legs hurt after the workout.)

Exercise 17.3 - Fill in the blanks with: ton, ta, tes:

1- Tu as oublié __ cahier. (You forgot your notebook.)

2- J'ai pris __ parapluie. (I took your umbrella.)

3- As-tu fais __ devoirs? (Did you do your homework?)

4- Puis-je emprunter __ calculatrice? (May I borrow you calculator?)

5- Il a vraiment apprécié __ aide. (He really appreciated your help.)

Exercise 17.4 - Fill in the blanks with: son, sa, ses:

1- J'adore __ robe. Elle lui va bien. (I love her dress. It suits her well.)

2- Il a oublié __ manteau chez moi. (He forgot his coat at my place.)

3- J'aime beaucoup __ sourire. (I like her smile a lot.)

4- Il est allé voir un film avec __ amis. (He went to see a movie with his friends.)

5- Il a acheté un cadeau pour __ mère. (He bought a gift for his mom.)

Exercise 17.5 - Fill in the blanks with: notre, nos, votre, vos, leur, leurs:

1- Vous avez une belle maison. J'adore particulièrement __ jardin. (You have a nice house. I particularly like your garden.)

2- Jeanne et Patrick emmènent __ fils au parc chaque jour. (Jeanne and Patrick take their son to the park every day.)

3- Nous allons avoir un repas de noël avec __ grands-parents. (We're gonna have a christmas meal with our grandparents.)

4- Pouvez-vous retirez __ chaussures? (Can you take off your shoes?)

5- Ils mettent __ valises dans la voiture. (They put their suitcases in the car.)

With those exercises out of the way, let's move on to the next: **demonstrative adjectives**.

In the words of the wise (also known as the internet): haters gonna hate, potatoes gonna potate. And we might as well add that possessives gonna possess, and demonstratives gonna demonstrate.

In short, the words themselves will already tell you what they do (Get it? No rocket science here, seriously)

Here are some things to fill you in about demonstrative adjectives:

- Demonstrative adjectives are used to point out something. In English, these are the words: this, that, these, and those. (e.g., this book, that face, these goosebumps, and those creatures.)
- In French, the word **ce** covers demonstrative adjectives in its entirety. This will, however, change its form depending on the kind of noun.
  - Singular masculine – **ce (cet*)**
  - Singular feminine – **cette**
  - Both means **this** or **that**
  - Plural masculine – **ces**
  - Plural feminine – **ces**
  - Both means **these** or **those**

*cet is used for singular masculine nouns that begin with either a vowel or a h.

- Important items to remember when using **ce**:
  1. **ce** always comes BEFORE the noun it is referring to, no matter what its form is.
  2. -ci is added at the end of the noun to point out its nearness to you. **-là** is added at the end of the noun to point out that it is far from you.

Track 47

Example: Prends cette valise-ci. (Take this case.)

Est-ce que tu reconnais cette personne-là? (Do you recognize that person?)

..and with that we're done for the day (hooray!)

But wait, here are some more exercises.

Exercise 17.6 - Fill in the blanks with: ce, cet, cette, ces :

1- __ appartement est spacieux. (This apartment is spacious.)

2- J'aime la couleur de __ rideaux. (I love the color of these curtains.)

3- J'ai vu __ groupe de musique en concert la semaine dernière. (I saw this music band in concert last week.)

4- __ banane est délicieuse. (This banana is delicious.)

5- Sandra a commencé à faire du sport __ dernières années. (Sandra started working out these last years.)

LET'S PRACTICE SOME MORE!

Exercise 17.7

I. **Possessive Adjectives - Fill in the blanks with the correct possessive determiner.**

1- _____ famille est intéressante. (my)

2- _____ neveux sont ici. (your)

3- Jean, David et Julie sont _____ amis. (my)

4- _____ amour est éternel. (their)

5- _____ visite me fait plaisir (your)

II. **Demonstrative Adjectives - Fill in the blank with the correct demonstrative determiner: ce, cet, cette, or ces.**

1- Tu as vu le film _____ matin?

2- Je suis folle de ('crazy about') _____ animal!

3- Qui est _____ jolie fille?

4- Que faites-vous _____ après-midi?

5- _____ enfants sont naïfs!

> **Fun fact:** *Every first Wednesday in France, a war siren is sounded as a practice or rehearsal. If the alarm sounds on a day other than Wednesday, that means France is at war from that moment on.*

Exercise 17.8 - Fill in the blanks with the correct possessive determiner:

1- J'adore __ nouvelle coupe de cheveux. Ça te va bien. (I love your new haircut. It suits you well.)

2- Le chien de mon frère adore __ balle de tennis. (My brother's dog loves his tennis ball.)

3- __ parents me donnent __ argent de poche chaque semaine. (My parents give me my pocket money every week.)

4- Jonathon porte __ espadrilles de course. (Jonathon wears his running sneakers.)

Camille offre un cadeau à __ mère pour __ anniversaire. (Camille offers a gift to her mother for her birthday.)

Exercise 17.9 - Fill in the blanks with the correct demonstrative determiner:

1- __ petits chiots sont très mignons. (These little puppies are very cute.)

2- Aidez-moi à porter __ armoire. (Help me carry this wardrobe.)

3- __ arbre a été planté par mon grand-père. (This tree has been planted by my grandfather.)

4- Ça fait une heure que je suis coincé dans __ embouteillage. (It has been an hour that I am stuck in this traffic jam.)

5- Peux-tu attacher __ guirlandes s'il te plait ? (Can you attach these garlands please?)

ANSWERS:

Exercise 17.1

1/ Ma 2. mon 3/ mon 4/ ta 5/ mon

Exercise 17.2

1/ Ma voiture est tombée en panne. 2/ Il a mangé mon yaourt. 3/ J'ai perdu mes lunettes. 4/ Ils m'ont acheté un délicieux gâteau pour mon anniversaire. 5/ Mes jambes me font mal après l'entraînement.

Exercise 17.3

1/ Tu as oublié ton cahier. 2/ J'ai pris ton parapluie. 3/ As-tu fais tes devoirs? 4/ Puis-je emprunter ta calculatrice? 5/ Il a vraiment apprécié ton aide.

Exercise 17.4

1/ J'adore sa robe. Elle lui va bien. 2/ Il a oublié son manteau chez moi. 3/ J'aime beaucoup son sourire. 4/ Il est allé voir un film avec ses amis. 5/ Il a acheté un cadeau pour sa mère.

Exercise 17.5

1/ Vous avez une belle maison. J'adore particulièrement votre jardin. 2/ Jeanne et Patrick emmènent leur fils au parc chaque jour. 3/ Nous allons avoir un repas de noël avec nos grands-parents. 4/ Pouvez-vous retirez vos chaussures? 5/ Ils mettent leurs valises dans la voiture.

Exercise 17.6

1/ Cet appartement est spacieux. 2/ J'aime la couleur de ces rideaux. 3/ J'ai vu ce groupe de musique en concert la semaine dernière. 4/ Cette banane est délicieuse. 5/ Sandra a commencé à faire du sport ces dernières années.

Exercise 17.7

Track 48

I. Possessive Adjectives

1/ Ma famille est intéressante. (my) 2/ Vos neveux sont ici. (your) 3/ Jean, David et Julie sont mes amis. (my) 4/ Leur amour est éternel. (their) 5/ Votre visite me fait plaisir (your)

II. Demonstrative Adjectives

1/ Tu as vu le film ce matin? 2/ Je suis folle de ('crazy about') cet animal! 3/ Qui est cette jolie fille? 4/ Que faites-vous cet après-midi? 5/ Ces enfants sont naïfs!

Exercise 17.8

1/ J'adore ta nouvelle coupe de cheveux. Ça te va bien. 2/ Le chien de mon frère adore sa balle de tennis. 3/ Mes parents me donnent mon argent de poche chaque semaine. 4/ Jonathon porte ses espadrilles de course. 5/ Camille offre un cadeau à sa mère pour son anniversaire.

Exercise 17.9

1/ Ces petits chiots sont très mignons. 2/ Aidez-moi à porter cette armoire. 3/ Cet arbre a été planté par mon grand-père. 4/ Ça fait une heure que je suis coincé dans cet embouteillage. 5/ Peux-tu attacher ces guirlandes s'il te plait?

Day 18: Direct and Indirect Object Pronouns

LESSON 18: Direct and Indirect Object Pronouns

By now you are probably already aware why pronouns were put upon this earth: they stand in place of nouns. Nouns can either be the subject or the object of a sentence, and pronouns being the stand-in for the nouns, can also be both.

Enter the direct object and indirect object pronouns.

So which is which and how do you know if it's direct or indirect?

- Direct objects are the persons or things that are the receiver of the action in the sentence.

- Direct objects answer the question 'who' or 'what'.

    I ate a sandwich. The <u>sandwich</u> is the direct object.
    I ate it. <u>It</u> is the direct object pronoun.

- Indirect objects are persons or things to whom or for whom the action occurs.

- Indirect objects are introduced by the preposition 'to' and 'for'. It answers the question to whom/for whom or to what/for what.

    I sang for the crowd. The <u>crowd</u> is the indirect object.
    I sang for them. <u>Them</u> is the indirect object pronoun.

Now, let's take a look at direct object pronouns in detail.

Here are the different direct object pronouns in French and their corresponding meanings in English.

1. **me** (or m' in front of a vowel or mute -h) This also means me.

2. **te** (or t' in front of a vowel or mute-h) This means you (second person singular – and used in talking to someone familiar to you or informally)

3. **le** (or l' in front of a vowel or mute-h) This means him/it (third person singular – masculine)

4. **la** (or l' in front of a vowel or mute -h) This means her/it (third person singular – feminine)

5. **nous** – This means us.

6. **vous** – This means you. Used for formal speech in the singular, or for both informal and formal speech in plural.

7. **les** – this means them

Remember:

- Because the pronouns stand in for the noun, you base the pronoun to be used on the gen-der and number of the noun you are replacing it with. For example, la mère (the mother) is a singular feminine noun, so it should be replaced with the direct object pronoun la.

Example:

> Je vois ma mère (I see my mother.)
> Je la vois. (I see her.)

- Direct object pronouns appear BEFORE the verb.

Now for the indirect object pronouns:

Meet the indirect object pronouns and their English counterparts.

1. **me** (or m' in front of a vowel or mute -h) This means me or to me.

2. **te** (or t' in front of a vowel or mute -h) This means 'you' or 'to you', and is used for singular informal speech.

3. **lui** – this means him or her; to him or to her.

4. **nous** – this means us or to us.

5. **vous** – this means you or to you, and is used in singular formal or plural formal and informal speech.

6. **leur**– this means them or to them.

Remember the following:

- Indirect object pronouns are similar to the direct object pronouns except for the third person singular and plural. Both *him* and *her* are **lui** in French, with no distinction between gender. Additionally, the third person plural is **leur**, regardless of the gender of the noun being replaced.

- Just like the direct object pronouns, indirect object pronouns usually appear before the verb.

- Example: Il parle aux fantômes. (He speaks to ghosts.) Il leur parle. (He speaks to them.)

In French, indirect object pronouns are used only for objects that are sentient (human or animals). For things, the adverbial pronoun **y** is used instead.

LET'S PRACTICE!

Exercise 18.1 - Select the right answer from the choices given:

1- Vous __achetez? (it) Are you buying it? **l'? les? le? la?**

2- Tu __ vois? (her) Can you see her? **la? elle? lui? le?**

3- Je ____ aime beaucoup. (them) I like them a lot. **leur? l'? leurs? les?**

4- Je cherche mon stylo, (it) __ était sur mon bureau. I'm looking for my pen, it was on my desk. **ce? c'? elle? il?**

5- Elle ____ demande de l'aider. (them) She asks them to help her. **leurs? lui? les? leur?**

Exercise 18.2 - Say if the <u>underlined</u> group of words is: a direct object or an indirect object:

1- J'aime <u>le fromage</u>. (I like cheese.)

2- Elle a entendu <u>son chien</u> aboyer. (She heard her dog barking.)

3- J'ai donné les clés à <u>Sandra</u>. (I gave the keys to Sandra.)

4- Tu peux prendre <u>mon stylo</u>. (You can take my pen.)

5- Il est allé à la fête pour faire plaisir à <u>sa femme</u>. (He went to the party to please his wife.)

> **Fun fact:** *In French New Year celebrations, there is a cake called Galette de Rois which made of puff pastry, flour, egg, rum and almond paste. A small plastic animal or toy is hidden in each cake. When family members share the cake, whoever finds the little gift in their slice is the lucky one.*

Exercise 18.3 - Replace the <u>underlined</u> group of words with the right direct object pronoun and rewrite the sentence:

1- Je mange <u>des fruits</u>. (I eat some fruits.)

2- Il a oublié <u>son manteau</u>. (He forgot his coat.)

3- J'ai passé <u>mon examen</u> avec succès. (I passed my exam with success.)

4- Claire amènera <u>sa voiture</u> pour nous chercher. (Claire will bring her car to pick us up.)

5- Lucien est allé rejoindre <u>ses amis</u> dans la cafétéria. (Lucien went to join his friends in the cafeteria.)

Exercise 18.4 - Fill in the blanks with : me, te, le, la, l', nous, vous, les :

1- Je te conseille d'acheter cette crème hydratante. Je __ utilise souvent et je trouve que c'est un bon produit. (I advise you to buy this moisturizer. I use it often and I think it's a good product.)

2- Nous avons eu un très bon serveur. Il __ a apporté notre commande rapidement et avec le sourire. (We had a very good server. He brought us our order quickly and with a smile.)

3- Je vais aller au musée du Louvre avec Benoit. Il va __ montrer la fameuse Joconde. (I am going to go to the Louvre Museum with Benoit. He's going to show me the famous Mona Lisa.)

4- As-tu reçu le colis ? je –'ai envoyé le Mardi dernier. (Did you recieved the package? I sent it last Tuesday.)

5- Où sont mes lunettes ? je __ ai cherchés partout. (Where are my glasses? I looked for them everywhere.)

Exercise 18.5 - Complete the sentences with the right direct object pronouns:

1- J'ai adoré ce film. Je __ ai vu la semaine dernière. (I loved this movie. I saw it last week.)

2- Il a pris ton parapluie. Il te __ rendra demain. (He took your umbrealla. He will give it back to you tomorrow.)

3- Il habite dans mon quartier. Je __ vois chaque matin en allant au travail. (He lives in my neighborhood. I see him every morning on my way to work.)

4- Mon chien est très énergétique. Il __ fait rire quand il court partout dans la maison. (My dog is very energetic. He makes me laugh when he runs all around the house)

5- Il va voir avec son supérieur et il __ rappellera. (He will see with his superior and he will call us back.)

Exercise 18.6 - Fill in the blanks with : me, te, lui, nous, vous, leur, y:

1- Notre chien a toujours faim. Ma sœur __ donne souvent à manger. (Our dog is always hungry. My sister often gives him food.)

2- J'adore ce restaurant. J'__ vais une fois par mois. (I love this restaurent. I go to it once per month.)

3- Le professeur __ rend nos copies d'examen. (The professor returns us our copies of the exam.)

4- Vas à la bibliothèque. Nous __ rejoindrons plus tard. (Go to the library. We will join you later.)

5- Je suis excité d'aller chez ma mère ce week-end. Elle va __ préparer mon plat préféré. (I'm excited to go to my mom this weekend. She will prepare my favorite dish for me.)

Exercise 18.7 - Replace the <u>underlined</u> group of words with the right indirect pronoun and rewrite the sentence:

1- J'ai envoyé une lettre <u>à mon ami</u>. (I sent a letter to my friend.)

2- Robert aime dire des blagues <u>à ses collègues</u>. (Robert likes telling jokes to his colleagues.)

3- J'ai donné un câlin <u>à ma mère</u>. (I gave a hug to my mother.)

4- Ils sont partis regarder un match de football <u>au stade</u>. (They went to see a game of football at the stadium.)

5- Il souhaite un joyeux noël <u>à toi et tes parents</u>. (He wishes a merry christmas to you and your parents.)

Exercise 18.8 - Complete the sentences with the right indirect object pronouns:

1- Les étudiants entrent dans la salle. Le prof __ rend leurs copies. (The students enter the classroom. The teacher gives them their copies.)

2- J'aime ma grand-mère. Je __ rends visite au moins une fois par semaine. (I love my grandma. I visit her at least once a week.)

3- Mon petit frère __ prend la main et __'emmène dehors pour voir la neige. (My little brother takes my hand and takes me outside to see the snow.)

4- Il __ donne la voiture à condition de __ la rendre avant midi. (He gives you the car on condition that you give it back to him before noon.)

5- Peux-tu __ rappeler cet après-midi ? (Can you call me back this afternoon?)

Exercise 18.9 - Replace the <u>underlined</u> group of words with the right pronouns and rewrite the sentence:

1- Je donne <u>mes clés à mon petit-ami</u>. (I give my keys to my boyfriend)

2- Il envoie <u>le ballon à ses enfants</u>. (He sends the ball to his children)

3- J'ai promis à <u>ma mère de prendre soin de son poisson</u>. (I promised my mother to take care of her fish)

4- Je passe <u>ma carte bancaire à la caissière</u>. (I pass my credit card to the cashier)

5- Sabine prête <u>sa boussole à Claude et Jamy</u> pour leur excursion. (Sabine lends her compass to Claude and Jamy pour they excursion)

ANSWERS:

Exercise 18.1

Track 49

1/ Vous l'achetez? 2/ Tu la vois? 3/ Je les aime beaucoup. 4/ Je cherche mon stylo, c'était sur mon bureau. 5/ Elle leur demande de l'aider.

Exercise 18.2

1/ A direct object 2/ A direct object 3/ An indirect object 4/ A direct object 5/ An indirect object

Exercise 18.3

1/ Je les mange. 2/ Il l'a oublié. 3/ Je l'ai passé avec succès. 4/ Claire l'amènera pour nous chercher. 5/ Lucien est allé les rejoindre dans la cafétéria.

Exercise 18.4

1/ Je te conseille d'acheter cette crème hydratante. Je l'utilise souvent et je trouve que c'est un bon produit. 2/ Nous avons eu un très bon serveur. Il nous a apporté notre commande rapidement et avec le sourire. 3/ Je vais aller au musée du Louvre avec Benoit. Il va me montrer la fameuse Joconde. 4/ As-tu reçu le colis? Je l'ai envoyé le Mardi dernier. 5/ Où sont mes lunettes? Je les ai cherchés partout.

Exercise 18.5

1/ J'ai adoré ce film. Je l'ai vu la semaine dernière. 2/ Il a pris ton parapluie. Il te le rendra demain. 3/ Il habite dans mon quartier. Je le vois chaque matin en allant au travail. 4/ Mon chien est très énergétique. Il me fait rire quand il court partout dans la maison. 5/ Il va voir avec son supérieur et il nous rappellera.

Exercise 18.6

1/ Notre chien a toujours faim. Ma soeur lui donne souvent à manger. 2/ J'adore ce restaurant. J'y vais une fois par mois. 3/ Le professeur nous rend nos copies d'examen. 4/ Vas à la bibliothèque. Nous te rejoindrons plus tard. 5/ Je suis excité d'aller chez ma mère ce week-end. Elle va me préparer mon plat préféré.

Exercise 18.7

1/ Je lui ai envoyé une lettre. 2/ Robert aime leur dire des blagues. 3/ Je lui ai donné un câlin. 4/ Ils sont partis y regarder un match de football. 5/ Il vous souhaite un joyeux noël.

Exercise 18.8

1/ Les étudiants entrent dans la salle. Le prof leur rend leurs copies. 2/ J'aime ma grand-mère. Je lui rends visite au moins une fois par semaine. 3/ Mon petit frère me prend la main et m'emmène dehors pour voir la neige. 4/ Il te donne la voiture à condition de lui la rendre avant midi. 5/ Peux-tu me rappeler cet après-midi?

Exercise 18.9

1/ Je les lui donne. 2/ Il le leur envoie. 3/ Je le lui ai promis. 4/ Je la lui passe. 5/ Sabine la leur prête pour leur excursion.

Day 19: The Subjunctive Mood

LESSON 19: The Subjunctive Mood

(and a little Q&A about it)

French subjunctive? What is it? If this is the first time you've heard of such a thing, don't worry, you're not alone.

So, question number 1: what exactly is it?

- The subjunctive is a grammatical mood which can be found in different languages, including

English and French. HOWEVER, it is so much more widely used in French than English.

- The subjunctive is used to **express varied states of unreality or uncertainty** - such as a judgment, wish, possibility, opinion, doubt, emotion, or something that has not yet occurred.
- You need to remember two things when it comes to what the subjunctive means:

SUBJECTIVITY and UNREALITY. If it can't be classified as either, you usually make use of the indicative mood.

- What's weird is, there is no future tense in the subjunctive, only past and present. If it is set to happen in the future, the present tense is used once again.

Question number 2: What is the subjunctive like in English?

- We use it when we say things like "If I <u>were</u> you" or "It is important that you <u>stop</u> to read the signs", and other similar subjective statements.
- The subjunctive often appears in subordinate clauses especially *that-clauses*.

Question number 3: When and where do you use it?

- In French, we use the subjunctive after certain words and conjunctions that have two parts and two different subjects. Example: *Nous voulons qu'elle* soit *heureuse*. (We want her to be happy.) The first part of the sentence uses nous as the subject, while the second part uses *elle*. Therefore, the subjunctive *soit* is used.

- The subjunctives usually appear after these verb types:

Track 50

Wishing something: **vouloir que** and **désirer que** (which means *to wish that or to want*) **aimer que** (meaning *to like that*), **aimer mieux que** and **préférer que** (which means *to prefer that*)

- fearing something: **avoir peur que** (which means *to be afraid that*)

- giving your opinion: **croire que** (which means *to think that*)

- saying *how you feel:*

  - **regretter que** (meaning *to be sorry that*)

  - être content que (meaning *to be pleased that*)

  - être surpris que (meaning *to be surprised that*) etc.

- The subjunctive may also appear in some expressions that begin with *il*.

○ Some examples:

    il faut que (*it is necessary that*)
    il vaut mieux que (*it is better that*)

Question number 4: How do you form the subjunctive?

- For verbs that end with -er, here is how you form the subjunctive: INFINITIVE minus -ER plus CORRECT ENDING.

- These are the endings to be added, depending on the pronoun it is being used with.

- For **je (j')**, add the ending **-e** (example: je donne)

- For **tu**, add the ending **-es** (example: tu donnes)

- For il**, elle, or** on, add the ending **-e** (examples: il donne, elle donne, on donne)

- For **nous**, add the ending **-ions** (example: nous donnions)

- For **vous**, add the ending **-iez** (example: vous donniez)
- For **ils** or **elles**, add the ending **-ent** (examples: ils donnent, elles donnent)
- For verbs that end with -ir, INFINITIVE minus -IR plus CORRECT ENDING.

These are the endings to be added:

- For **je (j')**, add the ending **-isse** (example: je finisse)
- For **tu**, add the ending **-isses** (example: tu finisses)
- For **il**, **elle**, or **on**, add the ending **-isse** (examples: il finisse, elle finisse, on finisse)
- For **nous**, add the ending **-issions** (example: nous finissions)
- For **vous**, add the ending **-issiez** (example: vous finissiez)
- For **ils** or elles, add the ending **-issent** (examples: ils finissent, elles finissent)

For verbs that end with **-re**, the subjunctive is formed by following this guide: INFINITIVE minus **-RE** plus CORRECT ENDING. The endings are same with that of the **-er** verbs.

LET'S PRACTICE!

Exercise 19.1 - Select the right answer from the choices given:

1- Je veux que tu (savoir) _____ la vérité. (I want you to know the truth.) **saves? savais? saches? sais?**

2- Bien que je (avoir) ___ mis un pullover j'ai toujours froid. (Although I've put a jumper on, I'm still cold.) **aies? avez? ai? aie?**

3- Il vaut mieux que tu (porter) _____ un costume. (It would be better if you wore a suit.) **portais? portez? portes? porte?**

4- Il est important que tu (aller) _____ tout de suite. (It is important that you leave right away.) **vailles? iras? vas? ailles?**

5- Ils veulent que je (ranger) _____ ma chambre. (They want me to tidy my room.) **range? rangez? ranges? rangie?**

Fun fact: *Horse meat, frog's legs and snails are delicacies for the French.*

Exercise 19.2: Conjugate "être" (to be), "avoir" (to have) and "aller" (tu go) in the subjunctive:

	Etre	Avoir	aller
que je			
que tu			
qu'il/elle			
que nous			
que vous			
qu'ils/elles			

Exercise 19.3 - Choose the correct answer:

1- Il faut qu'elle ___ courageuse. (She must be brave.)

   a. soit   b. est   c. soient

2- Je préfère que tu ___ chercher ma mère. (I prefer that you go get my mom.)

   a. vas   b. aille   c. ailles

3- Elle veut que je ___ des cours d'Anglais. (She wants me to take English classes.)

   a. pris   b. prenne   c. prennes

4- Il faut que vous me ___. (You have to believe me.)

   a. croyiez   b. croyez   c. croie

5- Choisis la chemise que tu ___. (Choose the shirt that you prefer.)

   a. préfère   b. préfères   c. préfèrent

Exercise 19.4 - Conjugate these verbs in the subjunctive:

1- Je veux que tu (savoir) ___ la vérité. (I want you to know the truth.)

2- Il est important que tu (sourire) ___ aux clients (It is important that you smile to the clients.)

3- Il faut que je (nourrir) ___ mon chien avant de partir. (I have to feed my dog before leaving.)

4- Il veut que nous (faire) ___ nos devoirs avant de regarder la télé. (He wants us to do our homework before watching the TV.)

5- Elle est contente que son fils (aider) ___ son père avec les travaux. (She is pleased that her son helps his father with the work.)

Exercise 19.5 - Conjugate "manger" (to eat), "partir" (to leave) and "croire" (to believe) in the subjunctive:

	Manger	**partir**	**croire**
que je			
que tu			
qu'il/elle			
que nous			
que vous			
qu'ils/elles			

Exercise 19.6 - Conjugate these verbs in the subjunctive:

1- Il faut que tu (faire) ____ de ton mieux. (You need to do your best.)

2- Je veux que nous (être) __ d'accord sur la couleur de la chambre (I want us to agree on the color of the room.)

3- Faut-il que je (sortir) __ après la réception ? (Do I have to go out after the reception?)

4- Il ne tolère pas que vous (parler) __ si fort. (He doesn't tolerate that you talk so loudly.)

5- Il ne voit pas très bien, il faut qu'il (mettre) __ ses lunettes. (He doesn't see very well, he must put on his glasses.)

ANSWERS:

Exercise 19.1

Track 51

1/ Je veux que tu saches la vérité. 2/ Bien que j'aie mis un pullover j'ai toujours froid. 3/ Il vaut mieux que tu portes un costume. 4/ Il est important que tu ailles tout de suite. 5/ Ils veulent que je range ma chambre.

Exercise 19.2

	être	**avoir**	**aller**
que je	sois	Aie	aille
que tu	sois	aies	ailles
qu'il/elle	soit	ait	aille
que nous	soyons	ayons	allions
que vous	soyez	ayez	alliez
qu'ils/elles	soient	aient	aillent

Exercise 19.3

1/ soit 2/ ailles 3/ prenne 4/ croie 5/ prefers

Exercise 19.4

1/ Je veux que tu saches la vérité. 2/ Il est important que tu souries aux clients. 3/ Il faut que je nourrisse mon chien avant de partir. 4/ Il veut que nous fassions nos devoirs avant de regarder la télé. 5/ Elle est contente que son fils aide son père avec les travaux.

Exercise 19.5

	Manger	**partir**	**croire**
que je	mange	parte	croie
que tu	manges	partes	croies
qu'il/elle	mange	parte	croie
que nous	mangions	partions	croyions
que vous	mangiez	partiez	croyiez
qu'ils/elles	mangent	partent	croient

Exercise 19.6

1/ Il faut que tu fasses de ton mieux. 2/ Je veux que nous soyons d'accord sur la couleur de la chambre. 3/ Faut-il que je sorte après la réception? 4/ Il ne tolère pas que vous parliez si fort. 5/ Il ne voit pas très bien, il faut qu'il mette ses lunettes.

Day 20: Conditionals

LESSON 20: Conditionals (and the lowdown on how they work)

You use conditionals, I use conditionals, all of us do – whether deliberately or not. It's ingrained in our daily speech, in either English or French.

So what is it, you ask?

It's a form of verb that we use when talking about things that may happen under certain conditions. In English we simply use the modal verbs 'would' or 'could' or its shortened form 'd, and then we add the main verb after it.

For example: I would wipe off that smirk on his face if my hand didn't hurt.

You wish it would be that easy in French, but it isn't.

First, let's look at the other uses of the conditional:

- To **ask politely** or formally, especially in public settings. (Example: I would like a cup of coffee, please.)
- To **say what you would like or need**. (Example: I would like to take a tour of the place.)
- To **make a suggestion**. (Example: I could come over and cheer you up.)
- To **give an advice to someone**. (Example: You should tell him you're sorry.)
- To **play roles, imaginary or not**. (Example: I would be the doctor and you would be the nurse.)
- To **nag or complain**. (Example: You could clean your room instead of sleeping around all day.)
- In "**even if**" or "**in case of**" clauses. (Example: Even if he were to sleep all day, he'd still get good grades.)

The basic rules:

- Most verbs in the conditional form follow this format: the infinitive (used as the stem) + an ending similar to that of the endings for the imperfect tense: -ais, -ais, -ait, -ions, -iez, and -aient.

- To put it simply, **INFINITIVE + IMPERFECT TENSE ENDING** equals a conditional form.

    For example: **donner** (to give) becomes:

Track 52

Je donnerais

Tu donnerais

Il/elle/on donnerait

Nous donnerions

Vous donneriez

Ils/ elles donneraient

finir (to finish) becomes:

Track 53

Je finirais

Tu finirais

Il/elle/on finirait

Nous finirions

Vous finiriez

Ils/ elles finiraient

Some changes in spelling for the conditional stem of regular -er verbs:

- The consonants 'l' and 't' in those verbs which end in -eler and -eter are doubled. The pronunciation of the first letter e also changes from 'uhr' to 'eh'. Exceptions are the words *geler* (to freeze), *peler* (to peel) and *acheter* (to buy).

Example: **appeler** (to call) becomes

Track 54

J'appellerais

Tu appellerais

Il / elle / on appellerait

Nous appellerions

Vous appelleriez

Ils / Elles appelleraient

- For verbs that end in -yer, the y often becomes i when used in the future tense.

Example: **nettoyer** (to clean) becomes

Track 55

Je nettoierais

Tu nettoierais

Il / elle/ on nettoierait

Nous nettoierions

Vous nettoieriez

Ils / elles nettoieraient

LET'S PRACTICE!

Exercise 20.1 - Choose the right form of the connector between brackets from the choices given:

1. Si nous avions de l'argent nous (donner) _____ à la Croix-Rouge. (If we had any money, we would give to the Red Cross.) **donneriont? donneront? donnerons? donnerions?**

2. Nous (aimer) _____ vous voir plus souvent. (We'd like to see you more often.) **aimeriont? aimerons? aimeriez? aimerions?**

3. Si tu m'aidais je (finir) _____ ce travail plus vite. (If you helped me I'd finish this job more quickly.) **finirait? finirai? finira? finirais?**

4. S'il n'était pas si cher je (commander) _____ ce manteau. If it wasn't so expensive I would order this coat. **commanderait? commanderiez? commanderais? commanderaient?**

5. S'il n'était pas fatigué je lui (demander) _____ de m'aider. If he wasn't tired I'd ask him to help me. **demanderais? demandera? demanderait? demanderai?**

> **Fun fact:** *In (very) exceptional cases, you can marry a deceased person with the permission of the President.*

Exercise 20.2 - Conjugate "être" (to be), "avoir" (to have) and "aller" (to go) in the present conditional:

	être	Avoir	aller
Je			
Tu			
Il/Elle			
Nous			
Vous			
Ils/Elles			

Exercice 20.3 - Choose the correct answer:

1- ___-je avoir un verre thé, s'il vous plait ? (Could I have a glass of tea, please?)

    a. Pourrait   b. Pourrai   c. Pourrais

2- Il ___ aller au Canada pour ses prochaines vacances. (He would want to go to Canada for his next vacations.)

    a. voudrais   b. voudrait   c. voudra

3- Si j'avais soif, je ___ de l'eau. (If I was thirsty, I'd drink some water.)

    a. boira   b. boirais   c. boirait

4- Si le ciel était moins nuageux, il ___ les étoiles. (If the sky was less cloudy, he would see the stars.)

    a. verrait   b. verrais   c. verra

5- En lisant ce livre, elle ___son français. (By reading this book, she would improve her French.)

    a. améliorerait   b. améliorerais   c. améliorera

Exercise 20.4 - For each sentence, say if the conditional is used: to ask politely, to say what you would like or need or to make a suggestion:

1- Pourrais-tu me passer le sel, s'il te plait? (Could you pass me the salt please?)

2- Je voudrais un peu de silence. (I would like some silence.)

3- Je devrais lui demander. (I would need to ask her.)

4- On pourrait prendre le métro pour y'aller. (We could take the metro to go there.)

5- Voudriez-vous venir avec nous ? (Would you like to come with us?)

Exercise 20.5 - Conjugate the verbs between brackets in the present conditional:

1- Je (aimer) ___ aller à la plage. (I would like to go to the beach.)

2- Nous (devoir) ___ partir parce que nous sommes déjà en retard. (We should leave because we're already late.)

3- Si vous aimez les haricots, vous en (manger) ___ souvent. (If you like beans, you would eat them often.)

4- Elles (aimer) ___ bien devenir des stars. (They would like to become stars.)

5- Je te (croire) ___ si ti me montres une preuve. (I would believe you if you show me a proof.)

Exercise 20.6 - Conjugate "manger" (to eat), "partir" (to leave) and "croire" (to believe) in the conditional:

	manger	Partir	croire
Je			
Tu			
Il/Elle			
Nous			
Vous			
Ils/Elles			

Exercise 20.7 - For each sentence, say if the conditional is used : to nag/complain or to make a suggestion:

1- On pourrait sortir boire un verre, si tu veux. (We could go out for a drink, if you want.)

2- Est-ce que ça te dirait d'aller au cinéma ? (Would you like to go to the movies?)

3- Tu devrais dormir au lieu de regarder la télévision. (You should sleep instead of watching the television.)

4- Si tu m'aidais nous finirons plus vite. (If you would help me we will finish faster.)

5- Il devrait faire plus attention à sa santé. (He should pay more attention to his health.)

Exercise 20.8 - Conjugate the verbs between brackets in the present conditional:

1- S'il faisait beau, je (aller) ___ me promener. (If it was sunny, I would go for a walk.)

2- Si tu faisais attention, tu ne (casser) ___ pas les verres. (If you were careful, you would not break the glasses.)

3- Si je gagnais au loto je (acheter) ___ une voiture. (If I won at the lotto I would buy a car.)

4- S'ils avaient du temps, ils (venir) ___ me rendre visite en été. (I they had time, they would come visit me in the summer.)

5- S'il cessait de pleuvoir, vous (pouvoir) ___ sécher votre linge. (If it stopped raining, you could dry your clothes.)

ANSWERS:

Exercise 20.1

Track 56

1/ Si nous avions de l'argent nous donnerions à la Croix-Rouge. 2/ Nous aimerions vous voir plus souvent. 3/ Si tu m'aidais je finirais ce travail plus vite. 5/ S'il n'était pas si cher je commanderais ce manteau. 6/ S'il n'était pas fatigué je lui demanderais de m'aider.

Exercise 20.2

	Etre	Avoir	aller
Je	serais	aurais	irais
Tu	serais	aurais	irais
Il/Elle	serait	aurait	irait
Nous	serions	aurions	irions
Vous	seriez	auriez	iriez
Ils/Elles	seraient	auraient	iraient

Exercice 20.3

1/ Pourrais 2/ voudrait 3/ boirais 4/ verrait 5/ améliorerait

Exercise 20.4

1/ To ask politely 2/ To say what you would like 3/ To say what you would need 4/ Make a suggestion 5/ Ask politely

Exercise 20.5

1/ J'aimerais aller à la plage. 2/ Nous devrions partir parce que nous sommes déjà en retard. 3/ Si vous aimez les haricots, vous en mangeriez souvent. 4/Elles aimeraient bien devenir des stars. 5/ Je te croirais si ti me montres une preuve.

Exercise 20.6

	Manger	Partir	croire
Je	mangerais	partirais	croirais
Tu	mangerais	partirais	croirais
Il/Elle	mangerait	partirait	croirait
Nous	mangerions	partirions	croirions
Vous	mangeriez	partiriez	croiriez
Ils/Elles	mangeraient	partiraient	croiraient

Exercise 20.7

1/ To make a suggestion. 2/ To make a suggestion. 3/ To nag/complain. 4/ To nag/complain. 5/ To make a suggestion.

Exercise 20.8

1/ S'il faisait beau, j'irais me promener. 2/ Si tu faisais attention, tu ne casserais pas les verres. 3/ Si je gagnais au loto j'achèterai une voiture. 4/ S'ils avaient du temps, ils viendraient me rendre visite en été. 5/ S'il cessait de pleuvoir, vous pourriez sécher votre linge.

Day 21: Adverbs

LESSON 21: Adverbs

Adverbs are some of the most hardworking words you'll ever find. They appear together with verbs, adjectives, and other adverbs, and give more information about when, where, how, or the extent to which and circumstances of something happening.

And oh, they pepper your speech too, making it sound more specific and a lot more colourful.

Here are some things you need to remember about adverbs.

HOW TO FORM ADVERBS

- French adverbs NEVER change their form! (hooray!) But there is one exception to this: the word **tout** which can change in some phrases.
- In English, just as in French, the adverbs are formed using the adjectives.
- In the same manner that most English adverbs end in -*ly* (beautifully, nicely, sweetly), a lot of adverbs end in -*ment*. This is formed through the feminine singular form of the adjective. The -*ment* ending is added to make it an adverb. Examples: *heureuse* becomes *heureusement* (which means fortunately, luckily or happily), and douce becomes *doucement* (meaning, slowly or gently).
- For adjectives that end in -é, -i, or u, the adverb ending to be added is also -*ment,* but the adjective to be added it to is the masculine form. Examples: *vrai* becomes *vraiment,* meaning, *truly* (note that the feminine form is **vraie**, but the masculine form is used instead)
- For adjectives that end in -*ant*, its adverb ending is -*amment*, while adjectives that end in

-*ent* use the adverb ending -*emment.*

- Some adjectives can also double as adverbs! These include *bon* (good), *mauvais* (bad), *droit*

(straight), and a few others.

Exercise 21.1 - Transform the adjectives between brackets into adverbs to complete the sentences:

1- (Général) ___, je n'ai pas cours le samedi. (Generally, I don't have classes on Saturdays.)

2- J'ai eu beaucoup de travail à terminer (dernier) __. (I had a lot of work to complete lately.)

3- Je me suis approché (doux) __ pour ne pas faire peur au chiot. (I approached slowly to not scare the puppy.)

4- Il a (complet) __ oublié notre rendez-vous. (He totally forgot our meeting.)

5- Le peintre passe son pinceau (lent) __ pour avoir une ligne droite. (The painter passes his brush slowly to get a straight line.)

Exercise 21.2 - Transform the adjectives between brackets into adverbs to complete the sentences:

1- Il faut conduire (prudent) ___. (You must drive carefully.)

2- J'attendais les prochaines vacances (Impatient) __. (I was waiting for the next vacations impatiently.)

3- Le temps semble avancer (Lent) __ à la fin de journée. (Time seems to move slowly at the end of the day.)

4- Elle a (Brillant) __ passé son test de conduite. (She brilliantly passed her driving test.)

5- J'ai (Clair) __ mal compris ce que vous m'aviez dit. (I clearly misunderstood what you have told me.)

WHERE TO PUT ADVERBS IN A SENTENCE

Unlike English, where adverbs can appear all over the place, the French adverbs are somewhat more structured and less unruly. Here are the important things for you to remember:

When modifying a verb:

• When short adverbs are used with verbs, the thing to note is whether there are one or more verb words. If there's only one (such as in the present or imperfect tenses), the adverb comes

AFTER the verb. Example: *Il pleut* toujours (It always rains).

- For verbs that consist of more than one word, such as the perfect tense, the adverb comes

BETWEEN the two verb words. For example: Elle a trop bu. (She has drunk too much).

- In some cases regarding adverbs that tell you how or where something is done, it usually comes AFTER the verb, regardless of the number of words in the verb. Alternatively, adverbs stating the specific time or day (*aujourd'hui* – today, *demain* – tomorrow, *hier* – yesterday) can be placed at the beginning or end of the sentence.

When used with an adjective or another adverb:

- Whenever an adverb modifies an adjective or another adverb, it usually comes BEFORE the word it modifies. For example: *Je suis* très *heureuse!* (I am very happy!) *C'est une femme* très bien *habillée* (That's a very well-dressed woman!)

In Negative statements:

- Adverbs used in negative statements come after the word **pas**. Example: *elle ne mange pas* **bien**. (She does not eat well.)

Exercise 21.3 - Transform the adjectives between brackets into adverbs to complete the sentences:

1- Il faut conduire (prudent) ____. (You must drive carefully.)

2- J'attendais les prochaines vacances (Impatient) __. (I was waiting for the next vacations impatiently.)

3- Le temps semble avancer (Lent) __ à la fin de journée. (Time seems to move slowly at the end of the day.)

4- Elle a (Brillant) __ passé son test de conduite. (She brilliantly passed her driving test.)

5- J'ai (Clair) __ mal compris ce que vous m'aviez dit. (I clearly misunderstood what you have told me)

LET'S PRACTICE!

Exercise 21.4 - Place the right adverb:

1. (Général) _____ ils passent la Journée de Noël chez les parents de sa femme. (They generally spend Christmas Day at his wife's parents'.)

2. J'ai lu des choses inquiétantes (dernier) _____ sur cet hôpital. (I've read some worrying things recently about that hospital.)

3. Faire revenir (doux) _____ la viande dans une cocotte. (Gently brown the meat in a pan.)

4. J'ai (complet) _____ oublié de donner à manger à son chat. (I completely forgot to feed her cat.)

5. Le professeur parle (lent) _____ aux étudiants. (The teacher talks slowly to the students.)

> **Fun fact:** *The word "France" means "land of francs." The Franks are Germanic tribes who lived in Northern Europe after the fall of the Roman Empire.*

ANSWERS:

Exercise 21.1

1/ Généralement, je n'ai pas cours le samedi. 2/ J'ai eu beaucoup de travail à terminer dernièrement. 3/ Je me suis approché doucement pour ne pas faire peur au chiot. 4/ Il a complétement oublié notre rendez-vous. 5/ Le peintre passe son pinceau lentement pour avoir une ligne droite.

Exercise 21.2

1/ Il faut conduire prudemment. 2/ J'attendais les prochaines vacances impatiemment. 3/ Le temps semble avancer lentement à la fin de journée. 4/ Elle a brillamment passé son test de conduite. 5/ J'ai clairement mal compris ce que vous m'aviez dit.

Exercise 21.3

1/ Il faut conduire prudemment. 2/ J'attendais les prochaines vacances impatiemment. 3/ Le temps semble avancer lentement à la fin de journée. 4/ Elle a brillamment passé son test de conduite. 5/ J'ai clairement mal compris ce que vous m'aviez dit.

Exercise 21.4

Track 57

1/ Généralement ils passent la Journée de Noël chez les parents de sa femme. 2/ J'ai lu des choses inquiétantes dernièrement sur cet hôpital. 3/ Faire revenir doucement la viande dans une cocotte. 4/ J'ai complètement oublié de donner à manger à son chat. 5/ Le professeur parle lentement aux étudiants.

Day 22: Relative Pronouns

LESSON 22: Relative Pronouns (qui, que, lequel, dont, où)

Relative pronouns are also relatively easy. These are the words who, which, that, whom and where, and we all use these in our daily speech.

The house <u>where</u> I grew up in was haunted by ghosts.

The lady <u>who</u> came over used to be a guy.

The sandwich <u>that</u> I ate earlier tasted like cardboard.

Here's what relative pronouns are used for:

- To point out and properly identify the person, place, or thing being referred to.
- To supply more information about the person, place, or thing being talked about.
- To connect the dependent clause or relative clause to the main clause.
- To replace the subject, direct object, indirect object, or preposition.

French relative pronouns work exactly the same way as their English comrades. These are the words **qui, que, lequel, auquel, duquel, dont and où**.

Now, let's take a look at each of these.

1. *qui* and *que*

Qui and **que** can both be used to refer to persons or things. The main differences are:

- *qui* is used for the subject (or indirect object for persons) and after a preposition (à, de or pour). It could mean *who, which*, or *that*.
- *que* is for the direct object and could mean *who, whom, which*, or *that*.

Examples :

Track 58

> Les amis que je vois le plus... (the friends that I see most...)
> ...la personne à qui il parle. (the person he is speaking to)

Take note : Qui and que strictly have separate uses and cannot be interchanged.

Exercise 22.1 - Complete the sentences with « qui » or « que »:

1- J'ai trouvé l'objet ____ tu as caché. (I found the object that you hid.)

2- Les vacances ____ j'ai prises m'ont fait du bien. (The holidays that I took did me good.)

3- As-tu vu le film ____ a gagné l'Oscar ? (Have you seen the movie that won the Oscar?)

4- L'homme à ____ je parlais est allé chercher de la nourriture. (The man I was talking to went to get food.)

5- L'animal ____ tu as vu n'était pas un renard. (The animal you saw was not a fox.)

2. lequel

Lequel is the French counterpart for 'which' and it is used for indirect objects. It follows the prepositions à, de or **pour** and only used when referring to <u>things</u> and never about people. Moreover, it has to agree with the noun's gender (masculine or feminine) and number (singular or plural).

- Masculine singular – lequel
- Masculine plural – lesquels
- Feminine singular – laquelle
- Feminine plural – lesquelles

Examples:

Track 59

> *le livre pour **lequel** elle est connue* (the book she isfamous for)

> *la table sur **laquelle** j'ai mis mon sac* (the table I put my bag on)

Take note that **lequel** changes into different words when combined with the prepositions à and **de**.

- à + lequel becomes auquel
- à + laquelle is still à laquelle (remains the same)
- à + lesquels becomes auxquels

- à + lesquelles becomes auxquelles
- de + lequel becomes duquel
- de + laquelle is still de laquelle (remains the same)
- de + lesquels becomes desquels
- de + lesquelles becomes desquelles

Exercise 22.2 - Complete the sentence with the right form of « lequel » :

1- ___ de ces robes est ta préférée? (Which one of these dresses is your favoutire?)

2- Entre tous ces bonbons, ___ tu voudrais? (Between all these sweets, which ones would you like?)

3- C'est le seul musée dans ___ on peut trouver ce genre d'expositions. (This is the only museum where you can find this kind of exhibitions.)

4- Le cours d'informatique ___ j'ai souscris est un peu compliqué. (The computer course I subscribed to is a little complicated.)

5- Elle pose son sac à dos ___ elle sort des feuilles et un stylo. (She puts down her backpack from which she gets out papers and a pen.)

Exercise 22.3 - Complete the sentences with « auquel » or « duquel » :

1- Le monsieur ___ je me suis adressé est très gentil. (The gentleman to whom I spoke is very kind.)

2- C'est le film au milieu ___ je me suis endormi, il était bien ennuyant. (It's the movie in the middle of which I fell asleep, it was very boring.)

3- Le tiroir ___ elle a sorti le carnet était plein à rebord. (The drawer from which she pulled out the notebook was full to the edge.)

4- L'homme devant nous est celui ___ j'ai vendu les lunettes. (The man in front of us is the one to whom I sold the glasses.)

5- Le chemin au bout ___ se trouve la pharmacie n'est pas très bien éclairé. (The path at the end of which is the pharmacy is not very well lit.)

3. *dont*

When translated in English, it means whose, of whom, of which. It may be used to refer to persons or things. The good news is, it does not change its form, nor does it have to agree with anything!

Some examples :

Track 60

les films dont tu parles (the films you are talking about) – plural

la femme dont la voiture est en panne (the woman whose car has broken down) – singular

4. où

This is used for places and times. Its English counterparts could be 'where', 'when' or even 'which' and 'that', depending on how it is used.

Some examples:

Track 61

Paris est la ville où on peut manger les meilleurs escargots. (Paris is the city where we can eat the best snails.)

C'est l'année où ils ont gagné la coupe du monde. (That's the year they won the World Cup.) In addition, où can also be used after prepositions.

La ville d'où elle vient... (The city where she's from...)

Exercise 22.4 - Complete the sentences with « dont » or « où » :

1- C'est l'artiste ___ tout le monde parle en ce moment. (It's the artist everyone is talking about right now)

2- Montres-moi tes affaires __ tu voudrais te débarrasser. (Show me your things that you want to get rid of)

3- La ville __ ils sont allés ne semblait pas très accueillante. (The city where they went didn't seem very welcoming)

4- Ça s'est passé la semaine __ il était parti en Irlande. (It happened the week he had gone to Ireland.)

5- Montres moi le restaurant __ tu m'as parlé l'autre jour. (Show me the restaurant you told me about the other day)

LET'S PRACTICE!

Exercise 22.5 - Choose the right pronoun:

1- Le théâtre est quelque chose ___ m'intéresse beaucoup. The theatre is something I'm very interested in. **lequel? que? dont? qui?**

2- La personne ____ ils parlent est un acteur célèbre. The person they're talking about is a famous actor. **qu'? dont? qui? lequel?**

3- Nos voisins ont un chien ____ nos enfants ont très peur. Our neighbours have a dog our children are very frightened of. **dont? de qui? duquel? que?**

4- Je connais quelqu'un ___ peut nous aider. I know someone who can help us. **que? qui? dont? lequel?**

5- C'est ton cousin ___ j'ai vu à la bibliothèque Was it your cousin I saw in the library? **laquelle? qui? dont? que?**

Fun fact: *France is the first manufacturer of wine in the world.*

Exercise 22.6 - Complete the sentences with the right relative pronoun:

1- Je connais quelqu'un ___ peut nous aider. (I know someone who can help us)

2- A __ as-tu donné la lampe du salon? (To whom did you give the living room lamp?)

3- La série __ je t'ai parlé est enfin sortie. (The show I talked to you about is finally out.)

4- La salle __ elle a mis ses affaires est fermée à clé. (The room where she put her belongings is locked.)

5- Le bâtiment __ il est sorti était une banque. (The building from which he came out used to be a bank.)

Exercise 22.7 - Choose the correct answer:

1- La voiture __ j'ai acheté est rouge. (The car that I bought is red)

    a. qui   b. que   c. laquelle

2- J'ai vu ma cousine aujourd'hui, __ tu as rencontré l'autre jour. (I saw my cousin today, which you met the other day)

    a. qui   b. laquelle   c. lequel

3- La voisine à __ tu as donné du sucre te remercie. (The neighbor to whom you gave sugar thanks you)

    a. que   b. qui   c. lequel

4- Le jeune homme __ le chien est malade est parti voir le vétérinaire. (The young man whose dog is sick has gone to see the vet)

    a. qui   b. lequel   c. don't

5- La boulangerie __ j'ai acheté ce croissant est fermée à cette heure. (The bakery where I bought this croissant is closed at this time)

    a. dont   b. où   c. lequel

ANSWERS:

Exercice 22.1

1/ J'ai trouvé l'objet que tu as caché. 2/ Les vacances que j'ai prises m'ont fait du bien. 3/ As-tu vu le film qui a gagné l'Oscar? 4/ L'homme à qui je parlais est allé chercher de la nourriture. 5/ L'animal que tu as vu n'était pas un renard.

Exercice 22.2

1/ Laquelle de ces robes est ta préférée? 2/ Entre tous ces bonbons, lesquels tu voudrais? 3/ C'est le seul musée dans lequel on peut trouver ce genre d'expositions. 4/ Le cours d'informatique auquel j'ai souscris est un peu compliqué. 5/ Elle pose son sac à dos duquel elle sort des feuilles et un stylo.

Exercice 22.3

1/ Le monsieur auquel je me suis adressé est très gentil. 2/ C'est le film au milieu duquel je me suis endormi, il était bien ennuyant. 3/ Le tiroir duquel elle a sorti le carnet était plein à rebord. 4/ L'homme devant nous est celui auquel j'ai vendu les lunettes. 5/ Le chemin au bout duquel se trouve la pharmacie n'est pas très bien éclairé.

Exercice 22.4

1/ C'est l'artiste dont tout le monde parle en ce moment. 2/ Montres-moi tes affaires dont tu voudrais te débarrasser. 3/ La ville où ils sont allés ne semblait pas très accueillante. 4/ Ça s'est passé la semaine où il était parti en Irlande. 5/ Montres moi le restaurant dont tu m'as parlé l'autre jour.

Exercise 22.5

Track 62

1/ Le théâtre est quelque chose qui m'intéresse beaucoup. 2/ La personne dont ils parlent est un acteur célèbre.

Track 63

3/ Nos voisins ont un chien dont nos enfants ont très peur. 4/ Je connais quelqu'un qui peut nous aider. 5/ C'est ton cousin que j'ai vu à la bibliothèque?

Exercise 22.6

1/ Je connais quelqu'un qui peut nous aider. 2/ A qui as-tu donné la lampe du salon? 3/ La série dont je t'ai parlé est enfin sortie. 4/ La salle où elle a mis ses affaires est fermée à clé. 5/ Le bâtiment duquel il est sorti était une banque.

Exercise 22.7

1/ Que 2/ Laquelle 3/ Qui 4/ Dont 5/ Où

Fun fact: *Horse meat, frog's legs and snails are delicacies for the French.*

LESSON 23: Reflexive Verbs (or when the subject and object are one and the same)

The interesting thing about the reflexive verbs (and the one thing that make them different) is that they make use of the same subject and verb. 'It' often appears in English together with reflexive pronouns such as *myself, himself, herself, or themselves.* (Example: *The cat cleaned itself.*)

'It is' basically works the same way in French, except that the reflexive verbs are more widely used compared to English.

Here are the important things to remember about French reflexive verbs:

- Reflexive verbs "reflect back" to the subject. (see the concept there?) This means the subject performs the action upon himself.
- A reflexive verb is made up of a reflexive pronoun and a verb.
- These verbs appear in the dictionaries as se + the infinitive form. Some examples:

Some examples:

Track 64

- **s'adresser à** - *to address, speak to*
- **s'approcher de** - *to approach*
- **s'amuser** - *to enjoy oneself*
- **s'appeler** - *to be called*
- **s'asseoir** - *to sit down*
- **se baigner** to swim
- **se brosser (les cheveux, les dents)** - to brush (one's hair, one's teeth)
- **se casser (la jambe, le bras)** to break (one's leg, one's arm)
- **se coiffer** to fix one's hair
- **se coucher** to go to bed

- **se couper** to cut oneself
- **se dépêcher** to hurry
- **se déshabiller** to get undressed
- **se doucher** to take a shower
- **s'énerver** to get annoyed
- **se laver** to wash

- Common things about reflexive verbs are: they all have something to do with body parts, personal state, clothing, hygiene, or location.

- Several reflexive verbs also have uses that are non-reflexive. Their meanings may also change slightly according to the usage.

How to form the reflexive verb in the present tense:

- First of all, you have to decide which reflexive pronoun to use. It could be any of the following:

Subject pronoun	Reflexive Pronoun	What It Means
je	me (m')	myself
tu	te (t')	yourself
il/ elle/ on	se (s')	himself / herself/ itself/ oneself
nous	nous	ourselves
vous	vous	yourself (formal)/ yourselves (formal or informal)
ils/ elles	se (s')	themselves

- The basic format looks like this: **subject pronoun + reflexive pronoun + reflexive verb.**

- The present tense form and the endings to be used remain the same: **-e, -es, -e, -ons, -ez, and -ent.** (See the lesson on present tense for more information).

- Some examples: je me lave (I wash myself), tu me laves (you wash yourself), il se lave (he washes himself), nous nous lavons (you wash yourselves), vous vous lavez (we wash ourselves), ils se lavent (they wash themselves).

- Please note that nous, vous, and se can mean two or more people and can be used to mean to each other or to one another. Example: les trois filles se ressemblent (the three girls resemble each other).

Exercise 23.1 - Conjugate "se laver" (to wash oneself), "s'amuser" (to have fun) and "s'asseoir" (to sit down) in the present tense:

	se laver	s'amuser	s'asseoir
Je			
Tu			
Il/Elle			
Nous			
Vous			
Ils/Elles			

Exercise 23.2 - Conjugate the verbs between brackets in the present tense:

1- Je (se lever) ___ très tôt chaque matin. (I wake up very early every morning.)

2- Il (s'installer) ___ à cet hôtel à chaque fois qu'il vient ici. (He moves to this hotel every time he comes here.)

3- Nous (se brosser) ___ les dents après chaque repas. (We brush our teeth after every meal.)

4- Tu (se laver) ___ les mains combien de fois par jour ? (You wash your hands how many times per day?)

5- Ils (se saluer) ___ très poliment. (They salute each other very politely.)

Where to put the reflexive pronoun:

• For present tense uses, the reflexive pronoun always comes BEFORE the verb.

• For negative commands (telling someone not to do something), the reflexive pronoun also comes BEFORE the verb.

• For positive commands, the reflexive pronoun comes AFTER the verb.

LET'S PRACTICE!

Exercise 23.3 - Choose the right connector between:

1- Je (s'asseoir) _____ dans le fauteuil. I sat down on the armchair. **m'est assis? me sont assise? me suis assis? me sont asseoir?**

2- Est-ce que tu (se brosser) _____ les dents? Have you cleaned your teeth? **t'es brossé? t'as brossé? t'est brossé? te suis brossé?**

3- Je (se décider) _____ à vivre en France. I've decided to live in France. **m'ai décidé? me suis décider? me suis décidé? me suis décidés?**

4- Il (se demander) _____ pourquoi elle était en retard. He wondered why she was late. **s'est demandées? s'est demandée? s'est demandé? s'est demandés?**

5- Je (se lever) _____ de bonne heure. I got up early. **m'ai levé? me suis levé? m'est levé? suis levé?**

Fun facts: *There is a street named after Victor Hugo in every town in France.*

Exercise 23.4 - Choose the correct answer:

1- Je ____ pour arriver à temps. (I hurry to arrive on time)

    a. me dépêche   b. me dépêches   c. tu dépêches

2- Vous ____ un gâteau ? (You're making yourselves a cake?)

    a. vous faites   b. nous faites   c. vous faisons

3- Il ____ souvent dans ce parc. (He often walks in this park)

    a. te promène   b. se promène   c. se promener

4- Les enfants ____ pour faire peur à leur père. (The kids hide to scare their father)

    a. se cache   b. se cachent   c. nous cachent

5- Vous ____ de la chanson de Julien ? (Do you remember Julien's song ?)

    a. se souvenez   b. vous souvenir   c. vous souvenez

Exercise 23.5 - Transform these sentences into the negative form :

1- Il se souvient de son enfance. (He remembers his childhood)

2- Je me brosse les dents après chaque repas. (I brush my teeth after each meal)

3- On s'appelle tous les jours. (We call each other every day)

4- Je me couche tard le soir. (I sleep late at night)

5- Je m'énèrve facilement. (I get angry very easily)

Exercise 23.6: Conjugate the verbs between brackets in the present tense :

1- On (s'amuser) ___ beaucoup ici. (We're having a lot of fun here.)

2- Il (s'approcher) ___ de moi et me dit « je t'aime ». (He gets closer and tells me « I love you »)

3- Je (se couper) ___ le doigt en préparant la salade. (I cut my finger while preparing the salad.)

4- Elle (se casser) ___ la jambe en tombant dans l'escalier. (She breaks her leg while falling down the stairs.)

5- Je (se déshabiller) ___ avant de prendre une douche. (I get undressed before taking a shower.)

ANSWERS:

Exercice 23.1

	se laver	s'amuser	s'asseoir
Je	me lave	m'amuse	m'assois
Tu	te laves	t'amuses	t'assois
Il/Elle	se lave	s'amuse	s'assoit
Nous	nous lavons	nous amusons	nous assoyons
Vous	vous lavez	vous amusez	vous assoyez
Ils/Elles	se lavent	s'amusent	s'assoient

Exercice 23.2

1/ Je me lève très tôt chaque matin. 2/ Il s'installe à cet hôtel à chaque fois qu'il vient ici. 3/ Nous nous brossons les dents après chaque repas. 4/ Tu te laves les mains combien de fois par jour? 5/ Ils se saluent très poliment.

Exercice 23.3

1/ Je me suis assis dans le fauteuil. 2/ Est-ce que tu t'es brossé les dents? 3/ Je me suis décidé à vivre en France. 4/ Il s'est demandé pourquoi elle était en retard. 5/ Je me suis levé de bonne heure.

Exercice 23.4

1/ me dépêche 2/ nous faites 3/ se promène 4/ se cachent 5/ vous souvenez

Exercise 23.5

1/ Il ne se souvient pas de son enfance. 2/ Je ne me brosse pas les dents après chaque repas. 3/ On ne s'appelle pas tous les jours. 4/ Je ne me couche pas tard le soir. 5/ Je ne m'énèrve pas facilement.

Exercise 23.6

1/ On s'amuse beaucoup ici. 2/ Il s'approche de moi et me dit « je t'aime ». 3/ Je me coupe le doigt en préparant la salade. 4/ Elle se casse la jambe en tombant dans l'escalier. 5/ Je me déshabille avant de prendre une douche.

Day 24: Time, Duration, and Related Expressions

LESSON 24: Time, Duration, and Related Expressions

There is huge volume of vocabulary and expressions pertaining to time, but this lesson aims to narrow it down to the most important parts. Below are the words, phrases, and expressions that you should remember when it comes to stating time in French.

USEFUL WORDS AND PHRASES

How often? (frequency)

Track 66

- **une fois** - once
- **une fois par semaine** - once a week
- **deux fois par semaine** -twice a week
- **quotidien** - daily
- **tous les jours** - every day
- **tous les deux jours** - every other day
- **hebdomadaire** - weekly
- **toutes les semaines** - every week
- **mensuel** - monthly
- **annuel** – yearly

When did/will it happen? (relative time)

Track 67

- **avant-hier** - the day before yesterday
- **hier** - yesterday
- **aujourd'hui** - today
- **maintenant** - now
- **demain** - tomorrow
- **après-demain** - the day after tomorrow

- **la veille de** - the day before
- **le lendemain** - the day after, the next day
- **la semaine passée/dernière** - last week
- **la dernière semaine**- the final week
- **la semaine prochaine**- next week
- **il y a peu de temps** - a little while ago

Points in time / periods of time

Track 68

- **une seconde** - second
- **une minute** - minute
- **une heure** - hour
- **un jour, une journée** - day
- **une semaine** - week
- **un mois** - month
- **un an, une année** - year
- **une décennie** - decade
- **un siècle** - century
- **un millénaire** - millenium
- **le matin** - morning
- **l'après-midi** - afternoon
- **midi** - noon
- **le soir** - evening
- **le crépuscule** – dusk
- **l'aube** – dawn
- **la nuit** - night
- **minuit** - midnight

Exercise 24.1: Choose the correct answer :

1- ___, j'irais en vacances. (___, I will go on vacation.)

    a. La semaine dernière   b. La semaine prochaine c. Hier

2- Il a pris le train pour Londres ___ (He took the train to London ___.)

   a. hier   b. demain   c. le lendemain

3- Nous avons un grand match ___. (We have a big match ___.)

   a. la semaine prochaine   b. la semaine passée   c. la dernière semaine

4- Elle te rendra visite ___. (She will visit you ___.)

   a. avant-hier   b. après-demain   c. la semaine dernière

5- Il le fera ___. (He will do it ___.)

   a. Hier   b. la veille   c. maintenant

Exercise 24.2 - Translate the words from English to French:

1- A day

2- A week

3- A month

4- A year

5- Once

Prepositions about time

à – used when expressing the time when a certain action will occur. (example: à 8 heures. At 8 o'clock.)

en – used when expressing the length of time, season, month, or year. (example: en été. In summer.)

dans – used when telling the amount of time before an action will happen. (Nous mangerons dans 10 minutes. We'll eat in 10 minutes.)

depuis – used when saying the duration of an ongoing activity. (Nous parlons depuis une heure. We've been talking for an hour.)

pendant/durant – refers to the entire duration of an action. (il a dormi pendant/durant 12 heures. He slept for 12 hours.)

pour – refers to the duration of a future event. (Il va parler pour une heure. He's going to speak for an hour.)

Exercise 24.3 - Complete the sentences with : "à", "en" or "dans" :

1- Je me réveille ____ 8 heures tous les matins. (I wake up at 8 o'clock every morning)

2- Elle a fini son travail __ l'aube. (She finished her work at dawn)

3- __ hiver, les arbres perdent leur feuillage. (In winter, trees lose their foliage)

4- Je terminerai ma formation __ une semaine. (I will finish my training in a week)

5- Je serais là-bas __ une minute. (I'll be there in a minute)

Exercise 24.4 - Complete the sentences with: "depuis" "pendant" or "pour" :

1- je l'attends ici ____ une heure. (I have been waiting for him here for an hour.)

2- Il peut tenir sa respiration sous l'eau __ trois minutes. (He can hold his breath under water for three minutes)

3- Il a voyagé __ un mois. (He traveled for a month)

4- J'ai encore du travail __ deux heures. (I still have work for two hours)

5- Elle attend une réponse __ hier. (She's been waiting for an answer since yesterday.)

LET'S PRACTICE!

Exercise: 24.5 - Choose the right answer:

1- 1 Je préfère voyager _____ été. a) dans b) en

2- 2 Elle va partir pour l'université _____ deux mois. a) dans b) en

3- Je dois m'en aller _____ quelques minutes. a) dans b) en

4- Je vais commencer mes devoirs _____ dix minutes. a) dans b) en

5- Il s'est rasé _____ deux minutes.

Fun fact: *April Fool's Day is believed to have originated in France, in 1564, when the country started following the Gregorian Calendar. Those that did not know about the change in the calendar were mocked as they continued to believe that the 1st of April was the first day of the French new year.*

Exercise 24.6 - Complete the sentences with the right preposition:

1- ___ été, il fait très chaud. (In summer, it's very hot)

2- Je vis ici __ une année. (I've been living here for a year)

3- À minuit, toutes lumières sont éteintes. (At midnight, all lights are off.)

4- Votre repas sera prêt __ dix minutes. (Your meal will be ready in ten minutes)

5- J'ai joué au football __ des années. (I played football for years)

ANSWERS:

Exercise 24.1

1/ La semaine prochaine 2/ Le lendemain 3/ La semaine prochaine 4/ Après-demain 5/ La veille

Exercise 24.2

1/ Un jour/Une journée 2/ Une semaine 3/ Un mois 4/ Une année 5/ Une fois

Exercise 24.3

1/ Je me réveille à 8 heures tous les matins. 2/ Elle a fini son travail à l'aube. 3/ En hiver, les arbres perdent leur feuillage. 4/ Je terminerai ma formation dans une semaine. 5/ Je serais là-bas dans une minute.

Exercise 24.4

1/ Je l'attends ici depuis une heure. 2/ Il peut tenir sa respiration sous l'eau pour trois minutes. 3/ Il a voyagé pendant un mois. 4/ J'ai encore du travail pour deux heures. 5/ Elle attend une réponse depuis hier.

Exercise: 24.5

Track 69

1/ Je préfère voyager en été. 2/ Elle va partir pour l'université dans deux mois. 3/ Je dois m'en aller dans quelques minutes. 4/ Je vais commencer mes devoirs dans dix minutes. 5/ Il s'est rasé en deux minutes.

Exercise 24.6

1/ En été, il fait très chaud. 2/ Je vis ici depuis une année. 3/ À minuit, toutes lumières sont éteintes. 4/ Votre repas sera prêt dans dix minutes. 5/ J'ai joué au football pendant/durant des années.

Day 25: Stressed Pronouns

LESSON 25: Stressed Pronouns

In the previous lessons, we talked about the other kinds of pronouns. Guess what? There's another type of pronoun I would like to introduce to you:

STRESSED PRONOUNS!!! *(ta-daaah!)*

What are these and what do they do???

Will it make you stressed out? No.

Are these pronouns stressed and overworked? Um, no.

Here's what they are:

- They come after prepositions such as avec (with), pour (for), sans (without), chez (at the house of), and so on. BUT ---
- They could also appear after **c'est,** or even alone!

In short, they are very flexible, have so many uses, and can be used anywhere in a sentence. (cooool)

Here are the different stressed pronouns:	
1. moi – me	5. nous – us
2. toi – you [singular informal]	6. vous – you [singular formal or plural formal and informal]
3. lui – him	7. eux – them [masculine]
4. elle – her	8. elles – them [feminine]

Some examples:

Track 70

Elle a peur de lui. She is scared of him.

Je pense à toi. I'm thinking of you.

Il va avec eux. He goes with them.

Here are the other uses of stressed pronouns:

- **To emphasize pronouns.** There's this thing called "accent tonique"(Tonic Accent) in French where they emphasise the words. In English, you normally just say the word more loudly or slowly, but in French, this won't do. In cases such as these, stressed pronouns are being used. This kind of speech will be more effective at drawing attention to the pronoun.

For example:

Je ne sais pas, moi.

This is kind of like saying "I don't know" but with considerably more feeling and emphasis on the I.

In a similar manner, it also appears after **c'est** or **ce sont** - also with the purpose of emphasizing the pronoun.

- **To point out a second subject or object in a sentence.** When there is more than one subject or object, the stressed pronoun comes to the rescue. Example: Je les ai vus, lui et elle. (I saw him and her.)
- **To ask and answer questions.** When asking questions like, "who wants to go?" This could be answered simply with a stressed pronoun. In the same way, you could also ask questions by using these pronouns, such as et toi? (and you?)
- **To take the place of indirect object pronouns in some cases where it cannot be used.** Some verbs just don't like indirect object pronouns, so you use a stressed pronoun instead. Example: Je pense à toi. (I'm thinking of you.)

LET'S PRACTICE!

Exercise 25.1 - Choose the right answer:

1- Elle a écrit l'histoire _____-même. a) elle b) lui c) soi

2- _____ aussi, il est fatigué. a) Il b) Lui c) Soi

3- J'espère que tu l'achèteras pour _____. a) je b) moi c) moi

4- _____, tu es intelligent. a) Tu b) Toi

5- C'est _____ (Jean) qui a dit la verité. a) il b) lui

> **Fun fact:** *Another interesting French fact is that a number of words in the English Language are derived from the names of prominent French individuals. For example, the word 'chauvinism' is believed to have originated from Nicola Chauvin, a soldier in Napolean's army whose loyalty to the emperor was legendary. The word 'sadism' originated from Marquis de Sade, a French nobleman who led the life of a libertine and wrote sadistic novels.*

Exercise 25.2 - Choose the correct answer:

1- ___ aussi, elle travaille ici. (She works here too.)

   a. Elle   b. Il   c. Lui

2- __ tu me comprends. (You understand me.)

   a. Toi   b. Lui   c. Moi

3- Pendant que __ il jouait, sa sœur faisait ses devoirs. (While he was playing, his sister did her homework.)

   a. Moi   b. Lui   c. Elle

4- Contrairement à toi, je lui fais confiance, ___. (Unlike you, I trust her.)

   a. Toi   b. Moi   c. Nous

5- Il va essayer de nous vendre de la contrefaçon, à ___. (He's going to try to sell us counterfeit, to us.)

   a. Lui   b. Nous   c. Eux

Exercise 25.3 - Complete the sentences with : "moi", "toi", "lui" ou "elle":

1- Chaque fois qu'il nous rend visite, elle se cache. Elle a peur de ___. (Every time he visits us, she hides. She's afraid of him.)

2- Elle ne m'a pas menti, ___. (She didn't lie to me.)

3- À __ il m'a dit qu'il voulait une nouvelle voiture. (He told me that he wanted a new car.)

4- On pourrait aller chez ___. (We could go to your place.)

   Il veut y aller sans ___. (He wants to go without her.)

Exercise 25.4 - Complete the sentences with : "avec", "pour", "sans" or "chez":

1- Tu as oublié tes clés ___ moi. (You forgot your keys at my place.)

2- J'ai acheté ce cadeau __ elle. (I bought this gift for her.)

3- Je ne parle plus à Marc. J'ai eu des problèmes __ lui. (I don't talk to Marc anymore. I had problems with him.)

4- Ils ont oublié de m'appeler et sont partis __ moi. (The forgot to call me and went without me.)

5- Ne sois pas timide, viens chanter __ nous. (Don't be shy, come sing with us.)

Exercise 25.5 - Complete the sentences with : "nous", "vous", "eux" ou "elles":

1- Venez avec ___. Nous allons au cinéma. (Come with us. We're going to the cinema.)

2- Elles sont très énergétiques. J'ai essayé de continuer la course avec __, mais je n'ai pas pu. (They are very energetic. I tried to continue the race with them, but I could not.)

3- J'ai apporté ces beignets pour __. (I brought these donuts for you.)

4- __, ils sont déjà montés sur la montagne. (They have already climbed the mountain.)

5- Mais vous avez une plus grande télévision chez __. (But you have a bigger television.)

Exercise 25.6 - Complete the sentences with the right stressed pronoun. :

1- Il est parti ce matin. Je n'arrête pas de penser à ___. (He left this morning. I can't stop thinking about him.)

2- C'est __ qui m'a aidé avec mon travail. (It's him who helped me with my work.)

3- Il a réparé sa voiture __-même. (He repaired his car himself.)

4- Etienne et Sandra sont déjà assis, mets-toi entre __. (Etienne and Sandra are already seated, sit down between them.)

5- Je crois qu'il faut aller le voir. Et __, t'en penses quoi ? (I think we have to go see him. And what do you think?)

ANSWERS:

Exercise 25.1

Track 71

1/ Elle a écrit l'histoire elle-même. 2/ Lui aussi, il est fatigué. 3/ J'espère que tu l'achèteras pour moi 4/ Toi, tu es intelligent. 5/ C'est lui (Jean) qui a dit la verité.

Exercise 25.2

1/ Elle 2/ Toi 3/ Lui 4/ Moi 5/ Nous

Exercise 25.3

1/ Chaque fois qu'il nous rend visite, elle se cache. Elle a peur de lui. 2/ Elle ne m'a pas menti, elle. 3/ À moi il m'a dit qu'il voulait une nouvelle voiture. 4/ On pourrait aller chez toi. 5/ Il veut y aller sans elle.

Exercise 25.4

1/ Tu as oublié tes clés chez moi. 2/ J'ai acheté ce cadeau pour elle. 3/ Je ne parle plus à Marc. J'ai eu des problèmes avec lui. 4/ Ils ont oublié de m'appeler et sont partis sans moi. 5/ Ne sois pas timide, viens chanter avec nous.

Exercise 25.5

1/ Venez avec nous. Nous allons au cinéma. 2/ Elles sont très énergétiques. J'ai essayé de continuer la course avec elles, mais je n'ai pas pu. 3/ J'ai apporté ces beignets pour vous. 4/ Eux, ils sont déjà montés sur la montagne. 5/ Mais vous avez une plus grande télévision chez vous.

Exercise 25.6

1/ Il est parti ce matin. Je n'arrête pas de penser à lui. 2/ C'est lui qui m'a aidé avec mon travail. 3/ Il a réparé sa voiture lui-même. 4/ Etienne et Sandra sont déjà assis, mets-toi entre eux. 5/Je crois qu'il faut aller le voir. Et toi, t'en penses quoi ?

Day 26: Demonstrative Pronouns

LESSON 26: Demonstrative Pronouns

We already know much about pronouns and their function to replace a noun. In English, the following demonstrative pronouns are also used for this purpose: this, these, that, and those.

French demonstrative pronouns work the same way, but with the usual twist - they have to agree with the nouns they're replacing.

Here are the different demonstrative pronouns and the basic rules.

1. ce

• Ce goes together with the verb être which means to be.

Some examples:

c'est	(it's or that's)	c'est moi! (that's me!)
c'était	(it was, that was)	c'était mon frère. (that was my brother.)
ce sont	(it's, that's)	ce sont eux (that's them.)

• ce becomes c' when it comes before a verb that begins with either e or é.
• ce becomes ç' when it comes before a verb that begins with a.

Ce is used in the following 3 instances:

• To identify a person or thing, either in a statement or with a question word. (*Qui est-ce?* Who is it? *Ce sont eux.* That's them.)
• To go with an adjective that refers to an idea or statement that cannot be classified as masculine or feminine. (*C'est dangereux!* That's dangerous!)

To put an emphasis on the statement. (*Ce sont les enfants qui ont fait le gâteau.* It was the children who made the cake.)

Exercise 26.1 - Complete the sentences with : "c'est", "c'était" or "ce sont":

1- J'ai adoré la fête d'hier soir. ___ amusant. (I loved yesterday's party. It was fun.)

2- Hier, j'ai dansé pendant toute la soirée. ___ fantastique ! (Yesterday, I danced all night long. It was fantastic!)

3- ___ eux qui ont fait tout le travail. (They are the ones who did all the work.)

4- Regarde par la fenêtre! ___ magnifique! (Look from the window! It's beautiful!)

5- ___ fou comment le temps passe vite! (It's crazy how time flies.)

2. cela, ça, and ceci

• Cela and ça both mean 'it', 'this', or 'that', and could refer to either a statement, an idea, or an object. The difference between the two is that ça is the less formal one and often appears in everyday speech.

Examples:

Track 72

> **Cela dépend.** It depends.
> *Ça ne fait rien.* It doesn't matter.

• Ceci is not as commonly used as **cela** and ça. Its uses are to refer to something that hasn't been previously mentioned, or to show someone a certain thing.

Track 73

> **Lisez ceci**Read this.
> **Prends ceci.** Take this.

Exercise 26.2 - Complete the sentences with : "ça" "c'est" or "ceci":

1- La musique, j'adore ___. (Music, I love that.)

2- __ est mon album photo. (This is my photo album.)

3- ___ très gentil de ta part de m'accompagner chez moi. (It's very nice of you to accompany me to my home.)

3. celui, celle, ceux, celles

- Celui means 'the one', and the different forms you use when referring to its feminine and plural forms are below.
  - celui-masculine singular
  - celle- feminine singular
  - ceux - masculine plural
  - celles - feminine plural
- **Celui and its different forms are used in the following cases:**
- Before **qui**, **que**, or **dont**. (*Celui dont je t'ai parlé.* The one I told you about.)
- Before prepositions like à, dans, etc. (*Celui proche de la porte.* The one near the door.)
- With **de** to show that it belongs to someone.
- With the endings **-ci** and **-là** to indicate how far something is from you. Like the demonstrative adjectives, -ci is added to mean it is closer, -là if it is farther. (*celui-ci ou celui-là?* This one or that one?)

Exercise 26.3 - Complete the sentences with : "celui", "celle", "ceux", "celles":

1- Ces deux livres m'appartiennent. ____-là sont à rendre à la bibliothèque. (These two books are mine. Those are to be returned to the library.)

2- Tu vois les deux filles là-bas? ____ qui est à droite est ma sœur. (You see the two girls there? The right one is my sister.)

3- Ces gâteaux-là sont bons, mais ____-ci ne le sont pas. (These cakes are tasty, but these are not.)

LET'S PRACTICE!

Exercise 26.4 - Choose the right answer:

1- J'ai trouvé ce livre-ci plus intéressant que _____-là. I found this book more interesting than that one. **celui? ceux? celles ? celle?**

2- Je n'aime pas cette jupe-là. Je préfère _____-ci. I don't like that skirt. I prefer this one. **celles? celle? celui? ceux?**

3- Jean m'a montré sa voiture _____ qu'il vient d'acheter. (Jean showed me his car, the one he's just bought.) **celles? celui? ceux? celle?**

4- Cette voiture-ci est française et _____-là est anglais. (This car is French and that one is English.) **ceux? celle? celles? celui?**

5- Est-ce que tu préfères ces chocolats-ci ou ____-là? (Do you prefer these chocolates or those chocolates?) **ceux? celles? celui? celle ?**

Fun fact: *France is home to the Louvre, one of the largest art museums in the world*

Exercise 26.5 - Choose the correct answer:

1- Aujourd'hui, __est mon anniversaire. (Today is my birthday.)

    a. ç›   b. c'   c. celui

2- Arrête de rigoler. Je ne trouve pas __ amusant. (Stop laughing. I don't find this funny.)

    a. ça   b. c'   c. celui

3- __ qui n'a jamais manqué d'argent, ne peut comprendre. (The one who never ran out of money, can't understand.)

    a. c'est   b. ça   c. celui

Exercise 26.6 - Complete the sentences with the right demonstrative pronouns:

1- Cette voiture n'est pas ___ de ma mère. (This is not my mom's car.)

2- J'aime ce film, mais je préfère ___ qu'on a vu la dernière fois. (I like this movie, but I prefer the one we saw last time.)

3- Il fait froid aujourd'hui. ___ serait mieux de sortir demain. (It's cold today. It would be better to go out tomorrow.)

ANSWERS:

Exercise 26.1

1/ J'ai adoré la fête d'hier soir. C'était amusant. 2/ Hier, j'ai dansé pendant toute la soirée. C'était fantastique! 3/ Ce sont eux qui ont fait tout le travail. 4/ Regarde par la fenêtre ! c'est magnifique! 5/ C'est fou comment le temps passe vite !

Exercise 26.2

1/ La musique, j'adore ça. 2/ Ceci est mon album photo. 3/ C'est très gentil de ta part de m'accompagner chez moi.

Exercise 26.3

1/ Ces deux livres m'appartiennent. Ceux-là sont à rendre à la bibliothèque. 2/ Tu vois les deux filles là-bas? Celle qui est à droite est ma sœur. 3/ Ces gâteaux-là sont bons, mais ceux-ci ne le sont pas.

Exercise 26.4

Track 74

1/ J'ai trouvé ce livre-ci plus intéressant que celui-là. 2/ Je n'aime pas cette jupe-là. Je préfère celle-ci. 3/ Jean m'a montré sa voiture celle qu'il vient d'acheter. 4/ Cette voiture-ci est française et celle-là est anglaise. 5/ Est-ce que tu préfères ces chocolats-ci ou ceux-là?

Exercise 26.5

1/ cinq 2/ onze 3/ soixante et une 4/ quatre-vingt-treize 5/ quatre-cent

Exercise 26.6

1/ Cette voiture n'est pas celle de ma mère. 2/ J'aime ce film, mais je préfère celui qu'on a vu la dernière fois. 3/ Il fait froid aujourd'hui. Ce serait mieux de sortir demain.

Day 27: Numbers

LESSON 27: Numbers

Contrary to what you might think, French numbers are actually easy. Well, not too easy when you compare it with the English ones, but at least they look the same, right?

Now, when we say numbers in this lesson, what we really mean here are cardinal numbers. A quick refresher: cardinal numbers are used to tell us how many are there, or the quantity. The other kind of numbers – ordinal – tell us the position or the order in relation to other numbers (e.g. st, 2nd, 3rd, 4th and so on.)

Now first things first. Here are the numbers in French.

Track 75

1	un	*ung*
2	**deux**	*deu*
3	**trois**	*trwa*
4	**quatre**	*katr*
5	**cinq**	*sank*
6	**six**	*sees or see*
7	**sept**	*set*
8	**huit**	*wheat*
9	**neuf**	*neuf*
10	**dix**	*deece or dee*
11	**onze**	*ohn*
12	**douze**	*dooz*
13	**treize**	*trayz*
14	**quatorze**	*kat-ORZ*
15	**quinze**	*cans*
16	**seize**	*sayz*
17	**dix-sept**	*dee-SET*

18	dix-huit	dee-ZWEET
19	dix-neuf	dee-ZNEUF
20	vingt	vang
21	vingt et un	vang-tay-UNG
22	vingt-deux	vang-DEU
23	vingt-trois	vang-TRWA
30	trente	trongt
40	quarante	kar-AHNGT
50	cinquante	sank-AHNGT
60	soixante	swah-SAHNGT
70	soixante-dix	swah-shangt-DEE
80	quatre-vingt	katr-VANG
90	quatre-ving-dix	katr-vang-DEE
100	cent	sahng
1000	mille	meel
10 000	dix mille	dee meel
1 000 000	un million	ung mee-LYOHNG

The basic rules:

- From seventy to ninety, you have to do a tiny bit of addition and multiplication. Seventy is soixante-dix (60 and 10), eighty is quatre-vingt (four twenties or 4x20), and ninety is quatre-vingt-dix (literally, four-twenty-ten).

Examples:

- seventy-two is soixante-douze (sixty-twelve)
- seventy-nine is soixante-dix-neuf (sixty-ten-nine)
- eighty-two is quatre-vingt-deux (four-twenty-two)
- ninety-two is quatre-vingt-douze (four-twenty-twelve)
- You use **et** for the following numbers:
- 21 vingt et un
- 31 trente et un
- 41 quarante et un
- 51 cinquante et un

- 61 soixante et un
- 71 soixante et onze

- **You use hyphens for the following numbers:**
  - 17, 18, 19, 22 – 29, 32 – 39 up to 79, and then 80 – 99

In most instances, cardinal numbers are spelt out. Except for the following:

- In dates (Example: le 29 janvier 1950)
- In prices (Example: L'armoire coûte 449 euros. the cupboard costs 449 euros.)
- In weights and measures (Example: Vous pesez 56 kilos pour 1,70 mètre. you weigh 56 kilos for 1 meter 70.)
- In mathematical usage
- In percentiles
- In addresses and telephone numbers
- To say approximate numbers in French, we add -aine to the number. This is equivalent to saying "about" or "around" in English. Examples: *une dizaine* (about ten) *une quinzaine* (about fifteen)

To form ordinal numbers, simply use the cardinal number, drop the last letter **e** (if any), and add the suffix **-ième**. The only exception to this is *premier* (or *première* for feminine) which means first. For example, quatre becomes quatrième and six becomes sixième.

LET'S PRACTICE!

Exercise 27.1 - Choose the right answer:

1- 7th _____ seventh

setième? septièmme? septieme? septième?

2- 500 _____ five hundred

cinq-cent? cinq-cents? cinq cents? cinq cent?

3- 8 ____ eight

huis? huite? hui? huit?

4- 21 _____ twenty-one

vingt un? vingt et un? vingt-un? vingt-et-un?

5- 92 _____ ninety-two

quatre-vingt douze? quatre-vingts-douze? quatre vingt-douze?
quatre-vingt-douze?

6- Sophie a (5) ____ ans. Sophie is five years old.

deux? cinq? trois? quatre?

7- Le bébé a (1) __ an. *The baby's one year old.*

quatre? deux? trois? un?

8- 570 _____ five hundred and seventy

cinq cents soixante-dix? cinq cent soixante-dix?
cinq-cent soixante-dix? cinq-cents soixantedix?

Fun fact: *From the French Alps to the marvelous beaches lining the azure waters in the French Riviera, France is one of the most visited countries in the world. In 2007, it attracted as many as 81.9 million tourists. This number was greater than its population!*

Exercise 27.2 - Choose the correct answer:

1- Marie a (5) ____ ans. (Marie is 5 years old.)

a. cinq   b. six   c. cinquante

2- Il y'a (11) __ joueurs dans l'équipe. (There are 11 players in the team.)

a. dix-un   b. onze   c. un et un

3- J'ai fini par utiliser (61) ____ planches pour le parquet. (I ended up using 61 boards for the floor.)

a. soixante et un   b. soixante et onze   c. six et un

4- Il est né en (93) ____. (He's born in 93.)

a. neuvente-trois   b. quatre-vingt-trois   c. quatre-vingt-treize

5- Les réparations ont coûté (400) ____ euros. (The reparations cost 400 euros.)

a. quatre-cent   b. cent   c. quarante-dix

Exercise 27.3 - Translate these numbers from English to French:

1- Twelve

2- Twenty-two

3- Thirty-one

4- Forty-five

5- Fifty

Exercise 27.4 - Complete the sentences with the right ordinal numbers:

1- Je suis la (1st) ___ de ma classe. (I am the first in my class.)

2- Barack Obama est le (44th) ___ président des Etats-Unis. (Barack Obama is the forty forth president of the United States.)

3- C'est la (3rd) ___ que je perds aux échecs contre mon père. (It's the third time I lose in chess against my father.)

4- C'est son (13th) ___ mois sans cigarettes. (It's his thirteenth month without cigarettes.)

5- J'ai assisté au (72th) ___ anniversaire de ma grand-mère. (I attended my grandma's seventy second birthday.)

Exercise 27.5 - Translate these numbers from English to French:

1- Seventy-two

2- Eighty-five

3- Sixty-three

4- Ninety-four

5- One hundred

Exercise 27.6 - Complete the sentences with the right approximate numbers:

1- La prof a (about thirty) ___ de copies d'examen à corriger. (The teacher has about thirty exam copies to check.)

2- Nos poules ont pondu (about twelve) ___ d'œufs. (Our chickens laid about twelve eggs.)

3- Il y'avait (about fifty) ___ de feux d'artifices pendant le spectacle. (There were about fifty fireworks during the show.)

4- (about a hundred) ___ de personnes sont venu voir son film. (About a hundred people came to see her movie.)

5- Je serais chez toi dans (about fifteen) ___ de minutes. (I'll be at your house in about fifteen minutes.)

ANSWERS:

Exercise: 27.1

Track 76

1/ septième 2/ cinq cents 3/ huit 4/ vingt et un 5/ quatre-vingt-douze
6/ Sophie a cinq ans. 7/ Le bébé a un an. 8/ cinq cent soixante-dix

Exercise 27.2

1/ cinq 2/ onze 3/ soixante et une 4/ quatre-vingt-treize 5/ quatre-cent

Exercise 27.3

1/ douze 2/ vingt-deux 3/ trente et un 4/ quarante-cinq 5/ cinquante

Exercise 27.4

1/ Je suis la première de ma classe. 2/ Barack Obama est le quarante-quatrième président des Etats-Unis. 3/ C'est la troisième fois que je perds aux échecs contre mon père. 4/ C'est son treizième mois sans cigarettes. 5/ J'ai assisté au soixante-douzième anniversaire de ma grand-mère.

Exercise 27.5

1/ Soixante-douze 2/ Quatre-vingt-cinq 3/ Soixante-trois 4/ Quatre-vingt-quatorze 5/ Cent

Exercise 27.6

1/ La prof a une trentaine de copies à corriger. 2/ Nos poules ont pondu une douzaine d'œufs. 3/ Il y'avait une cinquantaine de feux d'artifices pendant le spectacle. 4/ Une centaine de personnes sont venu voir son film. 5/ Je serais chez toi dans une quinzaine de minutes.

Day 28: The Present Participle

LESSON 28: The present participle

We know the present participles as words ending in -*ing*, such as dancing, jumping, and singing. However, unlike its English equivalent, the present participle is not as widely used in French.

These are the different functions of the present participle in French:

- As a verb expressing an action that is related to the main verb of the sentence. (example:

Vivant près de la ville, je vais souvent. Living near the city, I go there often.)

- As a verb used together with the preposition en. (example: *Appelle-nous en arrivant chez toi.* Call us when you get home.)
- As an adjective that modifies a noun. (example: *le soleil couchant.* The setting sun.)
- As a noun (examples: *un gagnant* – winner, *un étudiant* – student)

Some rules to remember:

- To form the present participle of -er, -ir, and -re verbs, use the nous form of its present tense and replace the -ons ending with -ant. For example, *donnons* becomes *donnant, mangeons* becomes *mangeant, finissons* becomes *finissant*, and *attendons* becomes *attendant*.
- Present participles can never be used to form tenses. Neither can they be used to translate Eng-lish verb forms literally.
- The present participle cannot be used to talk about something you are currently doing. For that, you must use the present tense.
- When used as an adjective, the present participle has to agree with the noun it describes.

(example: *des chaises pliantes* – the folding chairs)

LET'S PRACTICE!

Exercise 28.1 - Transform the following sentences in this exercise:

Elle travaille et elle chante. ➔ Elle travaille en chantant.

1. Elle écoute Mozart et elle danse _____

2. Elle conduit et elle parle _____

3. Elle sort et elle ferme la porte _____

Exercise 28.2 - Choose the correct answer:

1- Nous discutons en ___ du thé. (We talk while drinking tea.)

   a. boire   b. buvons   c. buvant

2- Je me suis fait mal en ___ ma langue. (I hurt myself biting my tongue.)

   a. mordons   b. mordions   c. mordant

3- ___ ma glace rapidement, j'ai eu mal aux dents. (Eating my ice cream fast, I got tooth ache.)

   a. Mangeant   b. Mangeons   c. Mangions

4- ___ être sourd, il ne se retourne pas quand je l'appelle. (Pretending to be deaf, he does not turn around when I call him.)

   a. Prétendons   b. Prétendant   c. Prétendre

5- Je fais descendre le Ketshup en ___ la bouteille. (I get the ketchup down by shaking the bottle.)

   a. secouant   b. secouons   c. secouer

Exercise 28.3 - Transform these infinitive verbs into present participles :

1- Vivre

2- Couper

3- Dormir

4- Manger

5- Croire

Exercise 28.4 - Transform these sentences like the example below :

Example: Elle chante et elle danse. ==> Elle chante en dansant. (She sings while she's dancing.)

1- Il fait la cuisine et il danse. (He cooks and dances.)

2- Elle parle et elle rit. (She talks and laughs.)

3- Je parle et je dors. (I talk and sleep.)

4- Il parle au téléphone et conduit sa moto. (He speaks on the phone and rides his motorcycle.)

5- Elle rentre et s'excuse du retard. (She enters and apologizes for the delay.)

Exercise 28.5 - Complete the sentences with the present participles of the verbs between brackets:

1- Ce concours compte beaucoup de (participer) ___. (This contest has many participants.)

2- Nous cherchons des concepts (différer) ___ de ce qui existe déjà. We are looking for concepts differing from what already exists.)

3- J'étudie souvent le jour (précéder) ___ l'examen. (I often study the day before the exam.)

4- Il a perdu tout son argent le (miser) ___ sur le mauvais cheval. (He lost all his money betting on the wrong horse.)

5- Elle a eu tort (confier) ___ son secret à Bernard. (She was wrong confiding her secret to Bernard.)

Exercise 28.6 - Transform these sentences like the example below:

Example: Je vis à l'étranger. Ma famille me manque beaucoup. ==> Vivant à l'étranger, ma famille me manque beaucoup. (Living abroad, I miss my family very much)

1- Il a beaucoup de choses à faire. Il n'a pas le temps. (He has a lot of things to do. He doesn't have time.)

2- Je sors du magasin, je paye mes achats. (I get out of the store, I pay my purchases.)

3- Je prends mon courage à deux mains. Je lui demande de sortir avec moi. (I gather my courage. I ask her to go out with me.)

4- Elle souffre de diabète, elle doit faire attention à ce qu'elle mange. (She suffers from diabetes, she has to pay attention to what she eats.)

5- J'assiste à des formations en marketing. J'apprends beaucoup de conseils utiles. (I attend training in marketing. I'm learning a lot of useful tips.)

ANSWERS:

Exercise 28.1

Track 77

1/ Elle écoute Mozart en dansant 2/ Elle conduit en parlant 3/ Elle sort en fermant la porte

Exercise 28.2

1/ buvant 2/ mordant 3/ en mangeant 4/ Prétendant 5/ secouant

Exercise 28.3

1/ Vivant 2/ Coupant 3/ Dormant 4/ Mangeant 5/ Croyant

Exercise 28.4

1/ Il fait la cuisine en dansant. 2/ Elle parle en riant. 3/ Je parle en dormant. 4/ Il parle au téléphone en conduisant sa moto. 5/ Elle rentre en s'excusant du retard.

Exercise 28.5

1/ Ce concours compte beaucoup de participants. 2/ Nous cherchons des concepts différant de ce qui existe déjà. 3/ J'étudie souvent le jour précédant l'examen. 4/ Il a perdu tout son argent le misant sur le mauvais cheval. 5/ Elle a eu tort confiant son secret à Bernard.

Exercise 28.6

1/ Ayant beaucoup de choses à faire, il n'a pas le temps. 2/ Sortant du magasin, je paye mes achats. 3/ Prenant mon courage à deux mains, je lui demande de sortir avec moi. 4/ Souffrant de diabète, elle doit faire attention à ce qu'elle mange. 5/ Assistant à des formations en marketing, j'apprends beaucoup de conseils utiles.

Day 29: C'est and Il est

LESSON 29: C'est and il est

Two of the most important impersonal expressions you will come across in French are **c'est** and **il est**. You have probably heard them already as these are commonly used in giving general comments, such as:

Track 78

- **C'est magnifique!** (It's magnificent!) C'est la vie. (That's life.)
- **Il est intelligent.** (He is smart.)
- **Il est facile.** (It is easy.)

In English, c'est and il est could mean this is, that is, it is, or he/she is and they are.

WHEN AND HOW TO USE C'EST

- c'est can be used with nouns in this order: c'est + article + noun or c'est + article + adjective + noun.
  - ◦ Some examples: C'est une bonne idée! (That's a good idea!) and c'est la vie! (that's life!)
- c'est can be used with adjectives: c'est + adjective.
  - ◦ Some examples: c'est merveilleux! (That's wonderful!) and c'est affreux (that's dreadful)
- c'est can be used with names too: c'est + name.
  - ◦ For example: c'est Jacques (It's Jacques)
- c'est can appear with stressed pronouns: c'est + stressed pronoun or c'est + stressed pronoun

+ relative clause.

  - ◦ Examples: c'est nous (It is us.) c'est moi qui donne le signal (I'm the one who gives the signal.)
  - ◦ Take note that the verb would have to agree with the pronoun.

- c'est is also used with adverbs: c'est + modified adverbs.
  - Examples: c'est par ici (it's right here) c'est par là (it's over there)

Reminders:

- *C'est is supposed to become ce sont when used with a plural noun. But in most cases, it is still used as c'est in spoken and informal French.*
- *C'est is more informal than il est.*

WHEN AND HOW TO USE IL EST

- il est can be used with a noun pertaining to specific things such as religion, race, or profes-sion. Il est + noun (no articles or adjectives comes with it)
  - Examples: Il est français (He is French). Il est professeur (He is a professor).
- il est can be used with an adjective referring to a person: Il est + adjective.
  - Examples: Il est gentil (he is nice). elle est jolie (she is pretty)
- il est can also be used with time and expressions related to time: Il est + time or il est + time expressions.
  - Examples: Il est cinq heures (it is 5 o'clock) Il est top tôt (it is too early)
- il est is used with prepositional phrases: il est + prepositional phrase.
  - il est à l'aéroport (he is at the airport) Il est ici. (He is here)
- il est also appears in some impersonal expressions. This is similar to c'est but more formal.
  - il est bon d'être avec des amis (It is good to be with friends)

Remember:

Il est changes its form depending on the noun it is replacing. It could become elle est, ils sont, or elles sont, depending on how it is used.

C'est versus il est

Here are some key differences on their respective usage:

- Use c'est with an adjective that describes a situation, and il est with an adjective that describes a person.
- Use c'est with a noun that has an article or adjective (modified noun) and use il est with a noun that is unmodified.
- Use c'est with a modified adverb, and il est with an unmodified one.

- Use c'est for specific names of people.
- Use il est to cite the location of a person.
- Use il est with time.
- Use c'est in less formal speech.

LET'S PRACTICE!

Exercise 29.1 - Choose the right answer:

1- _____ impossible de trouver un bon emploi.

    a. C'est   b. Il est   c. A or B

2- Mais non, _____ impossible !

    a. c'est   b. il est   c. elle est

3- _____ moi qui ai trouvé la solution.

    a. C'est   b. Il est   c. Elle est

4- Non, mon frère n'est pas médecin ; _____ professeur.

    a. c'est   b. il est   c. A or B

5- Cet homme-là, _____ soldat.

    a. c'est   b. il est   c. A or B

> **Fun fact:** *Stilts were invented in France by shepherds who needed a way to get around in wet marshes.*

Exercise 29.2 - Choose the correct answer:

1- __ cinq heures du soir. (It's five o'clock P.M.)

    a. C'est   b. Il est

2- __ ma sœur qui a changé les draps. (It's my sister that changed the sheets.)

    a. C'est   b. Il est

3- __ moins cher que dans l'autre magasin. (It's cheaper than in the other store.)

    a. C'est   b. Il est

4- __ mignon ton nouveau chaton. (He is cute your new kitten.)

    a. C'est   b. Il est

5- __ impératif que tu comprennes ce que je dis. (It is imperative that you understand what I'm saying.)

    a. C'est   b. Il est

Exercise 29.3 - Complete the sentences with the right form of "il est":

1- ___ intelligente. (She is smart.)

2- ___ prêtes pour leur prochain match. (They are ready for their next match.)

3- ___ encore tôt pour aller nager dans la piscine. (It's still early to go to swim in the swimming pool.)

4- Mes cousins sont géniaux. ___ toujours présents quand on a besoin d'eux. (My cousins are awesome. They're always present when we need them.)

5- __ l'heure de partir. (It's time to go.)

Exercise 29.4 - Complete the sentences with the right form of "C'est":

1- ___ magnifique! (That's wonderful!)

2- ___ les deux derniers tickets. (These are the two last tickets.)

3- Prends quelques fraises. ___ celles que j'ai cueilli tout à l'heure. (Take some strawberries. These are the ones I picked earlier.)

4- Fais-le, ___ une opportunité qui n'arrive qu'une seule fois dans la vie. (Do it, it's an opportunity that comes only once in a lifetime.)

5- Viens dire bonjour, ___ Marc et Lucie. (Come say hi, it's Marc and Lucie.)

Exercise 29.5 - Complete the sentences with "C'est" or "Il est": (note : you can write both if both are correct):

1- ___ important de faire attention en traversant la rue. (It's important to be careful while crossing the street.)

2- ___ très généreux de ta part. (It is very generous of you.)

3- Je crois que ___ trop tard pour regretter cette décision maintenant. (I think it's too late to regret this decision now.)

4- Elle dit que ___ sa faute. (She says it's his fault.)

5- Ouvres la porte, ___ mon frère. (Open the door, it's my brother.)

ANSWERS:

Exercise 29.1

Track 79

1/ C'est / il est impossible de trouver un bon emploi. 2/ Mais non, c'est impossible! 3/ C'est moi qui ai trouvé la solution. 4/ Non, mon frère n'est pas médecin; il est professeur. 5/ Cet homme-là, il est soldat

Exercise 29.2

1/ Il est 2/ C'est 3/ C'est 4/ Il est 5/ C'est

Exercise 29.3

1/ Elle est intelligente. 2/ Elles sont prêtes pour leur prochain match. 3/ Il est encore tôt pour aller nager dans la piscine. 4/ Mes cousins sont géniaux. Ils sont toujours présents quand on a besoin d'eux. 5/ Il est l'heure de partir.

Exercise 29.4

1/ C'est magnifique! 2/ Ce sont les deux derniers tickets. 3/ Prends quelques fraises. Ce sont celles que j'ai cueilli tout à l'heure. 4/ Fais-le, c'est une opportunité qui n'arrive qu'une seule fois dans la vie. 5/ Viens dire bonjour, c'est/ce sont Marc et Lucie.

Exercise 29.5

1/ C'est/il est important de faire attention en traversant le rue. 2/ C'est très généreux de ta part. 3/ Je crois qu'il est trop tard pour regretter cette décision maintenant. 4/ Elle dit que c'est sa faute. 5/ Ouvres la porte, c'est mon frère.

Day 30: Singular and Plural Nouns

LESSON 30: Singular and Plural Nouns

Here are some of the most important things you need to remember about French nouns.

- French nouns have a gender. To properly use nouns, you have to know if it is masculine or feminine as it will affect your usage of: adjectives to modify it, pronouns to replace it, and articles that come before it.
- Adjectives, pronouns, and articles are also affected by whether a noun is in its singular or plural form. These three have to agree with both the count and number.
- For singular nouns, we use the articles *le* or *un* for masculine, and *la* or *une* for feminine.
- For plural nouns, we use *les* and *des*.

Forming plurals

- Most French nouns can be converted into their plural form by adding -s, just as in English.

Some examples: *le livre* (the books) becomes *les livres* (the books) while *un jardin* (a garden) becomes *des jardins* (gardens).

- For singular nouns that already end in -s, you no longer need to add an additional s. For example, *un fils* (a son) is *des fils* (sons) in plural form.
- For singular nouns that end in -x, there is no change in the form. For example, the plural form of *le prix* (the prize/price) is *les prix* (the prizes/prices).
- Some plural French nouns end in -x. These include:
  - plural forms of nouns that end in -eau such as *un chapeau* (a hat) which becomes *des chapeaux* (hats).
  - plural forms of nouns that end in -eu such as *un jeu* (a game) which becomes *des jeux* (games).
  - plural forms of some nouns that in in -ou such as *bijou* (a jewel) which becomes *des bijoux* (jewels).

- In using the word à with articles and nouns, remember the following combinations:
  - ○ *à* + *le* becomes au (*au professeur)*
  - ○ *à* + *les* becomes aux (*aux professeurs*) *de* + *le* becomes du (*du maison*)
  - ○ *de* + *les* becomes des (*des maisons*)

LET'S PRACTICE!

Exercise 30.1 - Choose the right answer:

1. Elle écrit ___ lettre. She's writing a letter. **de? une? des? un?**

2. On entendait des (voix) ____ dans la pièce voisine. Voices could be heard in the next room. **voixs? vois? voix? voies?**

3. ___ oiseaux chantent. The birds are singing. **Les? Le? L'? La?**

4. Ça sert à protéger ses (genou) _____. It serves to protect your knees. **genou? genous? genouz? genoux?**

5. Elle porte ___ lunettes de soleil. She's wearing sunglasses. **une? de? un? des?**

Exercise 30.2 - Choose the correct answer:

1- Il fait __ ménage. (He does the household chores)

    a. un   b. une   c. le

2- Nous irons acheter __ pizzas demain. (We will go buy pizzas tomorrow)

    a. les   b. des   c. de

3- Je n'aime pas __ soupe. (I don't like soup)

    a. la   b. le   c. un

4- Elle a pris __ bateau pour aller à l'Angleterre. (She took a boat to go to England)

    a. le   b. un   c. une

5- As-tu __ couteaux? (Do you have the knives?)

    a. des   b. unes   c. les

Exercise 30.3 - Complete the table below with the right form for each noun:

Singular	Plural
	Des livres (books)
Une maison (a house)	
Un chapeau (a hat)	
	Des chevaux (horses)
Un jeu (a game)	

Exercise 30.4 - Complete the sentences with : "le", "la" or "les":

1- J'ai oublié ____ clés de mon bureau à la maison. (I forgot the keys of my office at home.)

2- Il va garer ____ voiture près de la porte. (He's going to park the car near the door.)

3- Tu vas tout droit puis tu tournes à gauche après ____ rondpoint. (You go straight and then turn left after the roundabout.)

4- J'ai cherché ____ lunettes de soleil partout. (I looked for the sunglasses everywhere.)

5- J'ai déjà abandonné mes résolutions de ____ nouvelle année. (I already abandoned my new year's resolutions.)

Exercise 30.5 - Complete the sentences with : "un", "une" or "des":

1- J'ai offert __ fleurs à ma mère. (I offered flowers to my mother.)

2- Il a __ gros appétit. (He has a big appetite.)

3- Elle a __ crampes à l'estomac. (She has stomach cramps.)

4- Nous voulons faire __ tour du monde. (We want to do a world tour.)

5- Rappelles moi d'acheter __ nouvelle ampoule. (Remind me to buy a new light bulb.)

Exercise 30.6 - Complete the sentences with : "le", "la", "les", "un", "une" or "des":

1- J'écris __ lettre à mon correspondant. (I'm writing a letter to my pen pal.)

2- Chaque fois qu'il passe devant __ pâtisserie il doit acheter __ croissant. (Everytime he passes in front of the pastry he has to buy a croissant.)

3- J'ai acheté __ Lego pour l'anniversaire de mon neveu. (I bought Legos for my nephew's birthday.)

4- __ coucher du soleil est le meilleur moment de __ journée. (The sunset is the best moment of the day.)

5- Nous sommes partis faire __ promenade au bord de __ mer. (We went on a walk by the sea shore.)

ANSWERS:

Exercise 30.1

Track 80

1/ Elle écrit une lettre. 2/ On entendait des (voix) voix dans la pièce voisine. 3/ Les oiseaux chantent. 5/ Ça sert à protéger ses (genou) genoux 6/ Elle porte des lunettes de soleil.

Exercise 30.2:

1/ le 2/ des 3/ la 4/ un 5/ des

Exercise 30.3

Singular	Plural
Un livre	Des livres
Une maison	Des maisons
Un chapeau	Des chapeaux
Un cheval	Des chevaux
Un jeu	Des jeux

Exercise 30.4

1/ J'ai oublié les clés de mon bureau à la maison. 2/ Il va garer la voiture près de la porte. 3/ Tu vas tout droit puis tu tournes à gauche après le rondpoint. 4/ J'ai cherché les lunettes de soleil partout. 5/ J'ai déjà abandonné mes résolutions de la nouvelle année.

Exercise 30.5

1/ J'ai offert des fleurs à ma mère. 2/ Il a un gros appétit. 3/ Elle a des crampes à l'estomac. 4/ Nous voulons faire un tour du monde. 5/ Rappelles moi d'acheter une nouvelle ampoule.

Exercise 30.6

1/ J'écris une lettre à mon correspondant. 2/ Chaque fois qu'il passe devant la pâtisserie il doit acheter un croissant. 3/ J'ai acheté des Lego pour l'anniversaire de mon neveu. 4/ Le coucher du soleil est le meilleur moment de la journée. 5/ Nous sommes partis faire une promenade au bord de la mer.

Bonus!

BONUS TOPICS

I. Using c'est..que/qui sentence structure for emphasis

Highlighting something in your speech is quite easy when speaking in English: all you need to do is say the word slower or more loudly than the rest of the sentence. In French, this is called accent tonique or tonic accent, and one of the ways to use this is to change the sentence struc-ture by using c'est...que/qui.

Here's how:

- Instead of the usual subject + verb + object structure, you twist things around using c'est + noun/stressed pronoun + que/qui clause.
- For example, instead of saying elle aime Tom (she likes Tom), you say c'est Tom qu'elle aime which is equivalent to "it is Tom that she likes". This way, Tom is being emphasized.
- In place of the noun to be highlighted, you can also use stressed pronouns (see previous lesson about this). For example: C'est moi qui l'aime. (It is ME who likes him.)
- For an even more dramatic and highly emphatic way of saying things, you can make use of both specific noun and stressed pronoun. For example: Tom, c'est lui qu'elle aime! (It is Tom, it's him that she likes!)

II. Cardinal numbers versus ordinal numbers

The difference:

- cardinal numbers are used to tell us how many, or what quantity, there are. They are used in count-ing. Example, 1, 2, 3, 4 and so on.
- ordinal numbers tell us the position or the order in relation to other numbers. They are used in classifying things. Example, 1st, 2nd, 3rd, 4th and so on.

For more of this, check out the lesson for day 27 on numbers.

III. Dates and Days

How to say the date:

- • Use this format: C'est + le + day of the month + month.
- For the day of the month, you use the cardinal numbers 2 to 31.
- For the first day of the month, you use the ordinal number "1st". Or in French, premier which is abbreviated as "1er".
- Examples: C'est le 4 septembre 2013. C'est le premier novembre. C'est le 1er novembre.
- In informal speech, you can say "On est" or "Nous sommes" instead of "C'est".
- Examples: On est le 15 octobre. Nous sommes le premier mars.

The days of the week:

Track 81

Day	In French	Pronunciation
Monday	**Lundi**	luhn-DEE
Tuesday	**Mardi**	mahr-DEE
Wednesday	**Mercredi**	mehr-kruh-DEE
Thursday	**Jeudi**	juh-DEE
Friday	**Vendredi**	vahn-druh-DEE
Saturday	**Samedi**	sahm-DEE
Sunday	**Dimanche**	dee-MAHNSH

Note: unlike in English, the first letters of the days of the week (les jours de la semaine) aren't capitalised in French.

How to ask the date:

Track 82

Quelle est la date?	What is the date?
Quelle est la date aujourd'hui?	What's the date today?
On est le combien aujourd'hui?	What's today's date?
Quel jour sommes-nous?	What day is it?
Quand?	When?

IV. Telling the time

• How to ask the time

Say: Quelle heure est-il? It is pronounced as kell eurh eh teel? Meaning, what's the time? Or what time is it?

• The format

Il est (insert number of hours) heure(s) (insert number of minutes). This format applies to both 12—hour clock and 24-hour clock.

Examples:

Track 83

Il est une heure. It is one o'clock.

Il est cinq heures douze. It is twelve minutes past 5.

You can abbreviate the time by placing the letter h in between the time and minutes. For example: 9h37 for 9:37 and 10H00 for 10 o'clock.

If you are going to only write down the minutes, use mn after the number. For example: 37mn.

V. The Weather

Track 84

le temps – weather

la météo – weather forecast

To ask about the weather, you can say:

Track 85

Quel temps fait-il?

Possible answers :	
Il fait... (It's...)	du brouillard (foggy)
	nuageux (cloudy)
chaud (hot)	orageux (stormy)
froid (cold)	
frais (cool)	Il... (it's...)

beau (nice)	
mauvais (bad)	pleut (raining)
humide (humid)	pleut à verse (pouring)
du vent (windy)	neige (snowing)
du soleil (sunny)	gèle (freezing)

VI. The Different Seasons and Months

Track 86

le printemps (spring)	l'automne (autumn)
l'été (summer)	l'hiver (winter)

The months of the year:

Month	In French
January	janvier
February	février
March	mars
April	avril
May	mai
June	juin
July	juillet
August	août
September	septembre
October	octobre
November	novembre
December	décembre

VII. Expressing Quantity

Here is a list of vocabulary pertaining to quantities, weights, and measures.

Track 87

une bouteille de	bottle	un carton de	box
une cuillère à soupe de	tablespoon	une cuillère à thé / café de	teaspoon
un kilogramme de / un kilo de	kilogram	un litre de	liter
une livre de	pound	un mille	mile
un pied	foot	un pot de	jar, cup
un pouce	inch	une tasse de	cup
un verre de	glass	assez (de)	quite, fairly, enough
autant (de)	as much, as many	beaucoup (de)	a lot, many
bien de	quite a few	combien (de)	how many, much
davantage m	more	encore de	more
environ	around, approximately	la majorité de	the majority of
la minorité de	the minority of	moins (de)	less, fewer

CONCLUSION

You didn't think I would just end this book without saying goodbye properly, did you? Well, that's where you're wrong. Proper goodbyes are terribly important now that we have been through a lot of grammar-y stuff these last 30 days. That kind of huge thing warrants a heartfelt farewell.

So here are some points I'd like to add before we go our separate ways.

1. I'd love to hear from you! Would it be too much to ask what you think about this book? If you can spare a few minutes, do let me know your thoughts by sending an email to contact@talkinfrench.com. Not only would I be delighted to receive your response, I would also want to know how I could be of further help and how I could make an even better book for all French language learners.

2. I hope you will stick to the habit of learning French each day. In this book, I have neatly divided the lessons into small daily tasks for you, hoping that the learning habit will stick. Did it work? I sure hope it did.

3. Learning French can be absolutely hard. After teaching it for so many years, I truly get that, and that's why I have been labouring to make this book as unboring as I can. The key is to focus on the fun parts. Like making it your new hobby, for example. I'll be here to guide you as best as I can.

And so with that, we say our goodbyes.

A bientôt, mon ami!

Frederic

Audio download instructions

Copy and paste this link into your browser:

- https://www.talkinfrench.com/audio-grammar-beginner/
- Click on the book cover. It will take you to a Dropbox folder containing each individual file. (If you're not familiar with what Dropbox is or how it works, don't panic, it just a storage facility.)
- Click the DOWNLOAD button in the Dropbox folder located in the upper right portion of your screen. A box may pop up asking you to sign in to Dropbox. Simply click, "No thanks, continue to download" under the sign in boxes. (If you have a Dropbox account, you can choose to save it to your own Dropbox so you have access anywhere via the internet.)
- The files you have downloaded will be saved in a .zip file. Note: This is large file. Don't try opening it until your browser tells you that it has completed the download successfully (usually a few minutes on a broadband connection but if your connection is unreliable, it could take 10 to 20 minutes).
- The files will be in your "downloads" folder unless you have changed your settings. Extract them from the folder and save them to your computer or copy to your preferred devices, *et voilà* ! You can now listen to the audio anytime, anywhere.

About the Author

Frédéric Bibard is the founder of TalkInFrench.com.

He spent several years teaching French while traveling abroad and has since moved back to Paris to dedicate his time in developing fun and helpful French language resources.

He takes food seriously (he is French after all), but he complements it with a love of running which allows him to nurture his passion for good food while staying in shape.

Say hello to him at contact@talkinfrench.com or www.talkinfrench.com.